Worth MORE
Than This

Young People Growing Up in Family Poverty

23

Roker, Debi
Worth more than this: young people
growing up in family poverty

£8.95

Please return/renew this item by the last date shown.
Fines will be payable if items are returned late.
Thank you for using Castle Learning Resource Centre.

The Sheffield College – Castle Centre
Tel. 0114 260 2134

First published in 1998

The Children's Society
Edward Rudolf House
Margery Street
London WC1X 0JL

A catalogue record of this book is available from
The British Library.

ISBN 1 899783 19 9

Contents

Acknowledgements

A large number of people and organisations contributed to the research described here.

The author is grateful for grants to undertake the research from The Children's Society, the Esmee Fairbairn Trust, and the Royal Philanthropic Society (now RPS Rainer).

Patrick West, Helen Bush, and Nicholas Rose undertook many of the interviews with the young people, demonstrating great care, skill and sensitivity in doing so.

John Coleman from the Trust for the Study of Adolescence and Roger Smith from The Children's Society made valuable and insightful comments on early drafts of this report.

The Children's Society would like to thank the members of the Publications Advisory Group for their valued advice: Kathy Aubeelack; Nicola Baboneau; Ron Chopping (Chair); Sara Fielden; Barbara Fletcher; Judy Foster; Nicola Grove; Virginia Johnstone; Christopher Walsh.

A large number of youth workers, social workers, teachers and others helped to make contact with young people living with their families on benefits and in temporary accommodation. They are not named individually here in order to protect the anonymity of the young people concerned, but their assistance and enthusiasm is very much appreciated.

Finally, great thanks must be given to the 60 young people who participated in the study, who talked honestly and openly about their lives, and about their hopes and aspirations for the future. This report is dedicated to them, and to the many thousands of young people in the UK today who are also 'worth more than this'.

CHAPTER *1*

Introduction and methodology

For me it's about not being part of things, not having the money to live normally like other people. Everything I do or I want to do, even like really small things, is decided by money, or by not having it anyway. (14-year-old young woman)

This report is about the experiences of young people who are growing up in families living in poverty. The numbers of children and young people who are living in poverty in the UK has increased sharply in the last few decades. This introduction very briefly summarises some of the key work in this area. It begins by exploring how we understand poverty.

DEFINING POVERTY

One noticeable aspect of the literature in this area is a debate about what exactly poverty is (for a discussion see Alcock, 1993; National Youth Agency, 1996). A variety of definitions have been given:

A condition characterised by severe deprivation of basic human needs, including food, safe drinking water, sanitation facilities, health, shelter, education and information. It depends not only on income but also on access to services. (United Nations, 1995)

People, families and communities whose resources (material, cultural, and social) are so limited as to exclude them from the minimal acceptable way of life. (Hertfordshire County Council, July 1996)

Poverty means going short materially, socially and emotionally. It means spending less on food, on heating and on clothing than someone on an average income. However, it is not what is spent that matters, but what isn't. Poverty means staying at home, often being bored, not seeing friends, not going to the cinema...It impinges on relationships with others and with yourself...It stops people being able to take control of their lives. (Oppenheim, 1993b, p.14)

Smith (1990) suggests that there are three main uses of the term 'poverty'. First, it is used to mean absolute poverty, in terms of complete destitution and the absence of food, or medicine to prevent disease. Second, it can refer to relative poverty, where a person or family is described as poor because they have less than the average or normal standards of living in a society. Third, poverty by exclusion is described as not having the basic requirements of citizenship – an adequate diet, good health, access to transport, and the ability to participate in the community. (For further information about current conceptualisations of poverty see Becker, 1991; Roll, 1992; Kumar, 1993; Oppenheim, 1993a, b; Dennehy *et al.*, 1997).

It is clear that, although many different definitions of poverty exist, most current definitions extend the meaning beyond the absolute definiton, i.e. defining poverty as not having enough food to stay alive. They are thus similar to the 'poverty by exclusion' categorisation described by Smith (1990) above. In this report, this broad definition of poverty, including its effects on people's lifestyles and their degree of inclusion/exclusion from society, is used. In adopting this view of poverty, the authors agree with Oppenheim (1993a, p. 12) that poverty is therefore about

being denied the expectation of decent health, shelter, a social life and a sense of self-esteem which the rest of society takes for granted.

It is also clear, as Alcock (1993, p. 4) suggests, that

what commentators mean by poverty depends to some extent on what they intend, or expect, to do about it.

The research described here therefore aimed to focus on young people's perspectives, on how they see the influence of poverty on their lives, and on what changes would make a difference to them.

LITERATURE REVIEW

There is clear evidence that there has been an increase in the number of families living in poverty in the UK over the past few decades (Oppenheim, 1993b; Holman, 1994). Dennehy *et al.* (1997), for example, show that the UK has seen a dramatic rise in poverty and inequality compared to a number of other countries. These authors show that, out of 16 countries in the period 1967–1992, the UK had the highest percentage increase in inequality (30 per cent), and the same increase in rates of child poverty (see also Oldfield and Yu, 1993; Oppenheim, 1993a). Further, poverty is not evenly distributed. Those living in poverty include disproportionately large numbers of families from ethnic minority groups, single parents, parents with disabilities, and those living in particular geographical areas (Kumar, 1993; Oldfield and Yu, 1993).

The increase in rates of poverty has meant that large numbers of children and young people are now growing up in very difficult financial circumstances. Dennehy *et al.* (1997) demonstrate that there are now 4.2 million children living in poverty in the UK, which is one in three of all children aged under 16. The reasons for the increase in poverty are complex, but include high unemployment, the growth of low paid work, and rising costs.

There has also been an increase in rates of poverty amongst young people because of the changes to benefit laws in the late 1980s. The 1988 Social Security Act prevented 16- and 17-year-olds from claiming income support. It also made a lower rate of benefit payable to 18- to 24-year-olds (see for example British Youth Council, 1993; COYPSS, 1993). This left many of this age group in destitution, and led to a subsequent rise in homelessness.

Further, throughout the 1980s the numbers of children and young people living in poor quality housing or in temporary/bed and breakfast accommodation increased (National Children's Home, 1993b). In the ten years to 1989 the number of house repossessions trebled, and the National Housing Forum concluded that one in 13 houses in the UK was unfit for human habitation (British Medical Association, 1995). Clark (1996) demonstrates that children living in temporary accommodation are particularly at risk in terms of their health and educational development, and suffer socially and educationally from frequent moves (see also Barnardos, 1995). One of the aims of the research described here was therefore to include young people growing up in temporary and bed and breakfast accommodation.

There is now very clear evidence that living in poverty is associated with risks to the health and well-being of children and young people. Poverty increases the risk that a young person will experience accidents, respiratory illnesses, and mental health problems. It also increases the likelihood of a poor diet, and higher than average use of legal and illegal drugs (see for example Blackburn, 1991; Kumar, 1993; Dennehy *et al.*, 1997).

Blackburn (1991) identifies three key ways in which income can affect health and well-being. First, income is a health resource, influencing where people live, their standard of accommodation, access to work, leisure and health resources, and food, fuel and clothing. Second, poverty affects physiological processes, as those living in poverty have greater exposure to harmful things such as poor diet, infection, damp and cold. Third, poverty affects psychological and behavioural processes, reducing life choices, increasing feelings of powerlessness and lack of control, and increasing the likelihood of the use of coping strategies such as illegal drugs, alcohol and cigarettes. Growing up in family poverty therefore

(i) increases the risk of falling behind at school, leaving school early, and getting few or no qualifications;

(ii) increases the likelihood of involvement in offending, and being a young parent;

(iii) reduces young people's prospects for adulthood, with a reduced earning capacity and greater risk of unemployment.

There is now a burgeoning literature on poverty and its effects, and the reader is referred to these for a more detailed account than is possible here (see, for example, Oppenheim, 1993a; Dennehy *et al.*, 1997). A number of important points can be drawn, however, from the literature that is available on young people and poverty.

First, much of the work on the effects of poverty has focused on the experiences of adults living in poverty, or on families with young children, rather than on those with teenagers.

Second, much of the research on young people has centred on those who are homeless or estranged from their families (for example, National Children's Home, 1993a; COYPSS, 1993), rather than those who are living at home and growing up in family poverty. Much less is known about the experiences of this group, and the impact of poverty at a key time in a person's development.

Third, there have been few studies which have looked in detail at young people's experiences and their views about the effects of poverty on different areas of their lives. Rather, much of the information currently available has aimed to document the situation for large populations.

AIMS OF THE RESEARCH

The research described below therefore aimed to focus on young people's views and experiences, using their words wherever possible to describe the experience of growing up in family poverty. The aim was to focus on young people who were living with their parent/s, in families who are dependent on benefits. A further aim was to include young people in the same circumstances, but who were living in temporary or bed and breakfast accommodation.

COLLECTING THE INFORMATION

The information reported here comes from 60 individual interviews undertaken in 1996–1997 with young people aged 13–18. The young people were all in families which were dependent on benefits (though see Chapters 2 and 3 for further information about family income). In addition, seven young people, all in the south coast sample, were living in temporary or bed and breakfast accommodation.

The majority of the sample was white/European, with seven individuals from African-Caribbean, Asian, and Middle Eastern families. In terms of gender, 28 of the young people were female, and 32 were male.

The young people were living in a variety of family circumstances, in single-parent families, two-parent families, and step-families, the details of which are presented in Chapter 5. (Note that, for ease of reading, the word 'parents' is used throughout this report. This should be taken to include lone parents, natural parents and step-parents.)

SAMPLE SELECTION

In order to get information from young people living in a variety of circumstances and from a variety of backgrounds, the interviews were conducted in three different parts of the country – the south coast, the west of England, and the west of Scotland. Twenty interviews were conducted in each of these areas. These were undertaken by local interviewers, in order to have people doing the interviews who were familiar with the local area and with local issues.

The three areas from which the sample was drawn were very diverse.

The 'south coast' interviews took place across a wide geographical area, but mainly included young people living in seaside towns in East and West Sussex. Although including areas of considerable affluence, many of these towns had suffered serious decline during the 1980s, with high levels of unemployment in certain areas, high costs of living (particularly in relation to accommodation), and much poor quality housing. There were a large number of families living in temporary and bed and breakfast accommodation in this area, and all the young people in the study who were living in temporary accommodation lived on the south coast.

The 'west of England' interviews were undertaken mainly in Gloucestershire and Herefordshire. A number of the young people from this area who took part in the study lived in large, run-down housing estates; others lived in isolated rural communities, a long distance from the nearest town.

The 'Scottish' sample were drawn mainly from the Glasgow area, where many of the young people lived on large, poorly maintained housing estates, characterised by high rates of crime, unemployment and drug use. Scotland as a whole has experienced a steep rise in the numbers of families living in poverty in recent years (see for example Long *et al.*, 1996).

The young people were commissioned to take part in the study in a variety of ways, including via advertisements in youth clubs, word of mouth, and via social workers and youth workers. Parental permission was obtained for those aged under 16 who wished to take part. The interviews were held wherever the young person wanted, and took place in youth clubs, their homes, and in workers' offices. Each young person was paid £10 as a 'thank-you' for their time.

When their participation was being negotiated, the young people were assured that the information they gave was confidential to the research team. However, they were also told that in cases where they revealed abuse, the researcher might have to divulge this information to other professionals. They were also told that the information would be used, anonymously, in the final report on the research, and that it might also be published (and therefore publicly available) as a book.

THE INTERVIEWS

The interview questions were devised by the researchers in collaboration with those working with young people in a variety of settings. The interview was divided into nine sections. These are detailed below, with the question areas that were included in each section:

1 *Current situation and family income.* Who they live with, whether they have contact with both natural parents, how long since their parent/s have worked, type of accommodation and housing history, view of accommodation, knowledge of family income.

2 *Personal finances.* Amount of own income and sources of income, what they spend their money on, whether they have debts or savings, whether they give any of their income to their family, and whether there are things they think they should have but can't afford.

3 *Friends and social lives.* Where their friends live, where they meet them, how they spend their time, whether their income affects the leisure activities they engage in.

4 *Family relationships.* How they view their relationship with their parent/s, the cause of disagreements in the family, whether their parent/s are happy with how the young people are living their lives, and what their parent/s want for them for the future.

5 *Physical health.* Their view of their current health, sources of advice about health, dental health, food and income, use of legal and illegal drugs.

6 *School life and current activities.* What they are currently doing, view of school days, whether they had time off from school, whether they could not afford anything they needed for school.

7 *Crime and the law*. Involvement with the police and in crime, whether family/friends have been involved in crime, whether they have been a victim of crime.

8 *Future prospects and aspirations*. What they plan to do in the next few years, their view of whether they will be able to do this, age at which they plan to leave home.

9 *Psychological aspects*. How they feel about their life overall, whether they feel positive about the future, what they do when they need help and advice, their worries and concerns, view of current situation and life opportunities in comparison to others.

Each interview took between 45 minutes and one-and-a-half hours to complete, and was tape-recorded with the young person's permission. At the end of the interview, the young people were asked whether they had any questions, or whether there was anything they wished to discuss further. All the interviews were then transcribed.

STRUCTURE OF THE REPORT

The results of the interviews are described in Chapters 2 to 9, detailing the effects of poverty on young people's friends and social lives, family relationships, physical health, and aspirations and feelings (note that areas 8 and 9 above were combined). This is followed in Chapter 10 by an outline of the main themes that emerged in the majority of the interviews. Finally, in Chapter 11 a number of conclusions are drawn about the nature of the relationship between income, family life and young people's lives, and policy recommendations are made.

CHAPTER 2

Family accommodation, parents' employment history and income

This chapter focuses on the results from the first section of the interview, which explored the young people's accommodation history, their views about their accommodation, and their families' income.

TYPES OF ACCOMMODATION

The type of accommodation that the young people were living in is described in Table 1. As the table shows, the majority of the sample –

Table 1 *Type of accommodation the young people lived in*

Type of accommodation	Number of young people
Council-owned houses and flats	27
Temporary accommodation (hotel or bed and breakfast)	7
Privately rented accommodation	10
Own home	5
Caravan (temporary)	1
Did not know/no information	10

27 of the 60 – were living in council-owned houses and flats. In addition, seven young people were living in temporary accommodation provided by their local council, either in the form of hotel rooms, bed and breakfast accommodation, or a short-stay flat. Ten of the young

people were in privately rented accommodation, with five families owning their own home, each with a mortgage. One young person was living with their family in a caravan in the front garden, as their house had been badly damaged by fire. The remainder of the young people were not sure what type of accommodation they were in.

Approximately two-thirds of the sample had been living in their present homes for two years of more. The remainder of the young people had either moved recently or were expecting to move, generally from temporary accommodation to a council house, or to a larger property. It is of note that those who had moved most often during the last few years, or who were expecting to move soon, were from the south coast sample. The west of England and the Scottish young people usually had much more stable accommodation histories. The young people who were living in temporary accommodation were there as a result of domestic violence, failed businesses and bankruptcy, or eviction from privately rented accommodation.

The young people had mixed views about their homes. Just over a third of the sample described their homes in very positive terms, as 'really nice', 'lovely and warm', 'cosy', and 'huge, lots of space'. Another group of ten young people identified particular problems, such as damp, discoloured and peeling wallpaper, ill-fitting windows and mould on the walls. This group were mainly in private rented accommodation, and many described their families' long battles with landlords to try to get repairs and improvements done to their home. These young people often talked about how 'grotty' or 'disgusting' they thought their home was, and how embarrassed they felt about it. They also commented on how this affected their social lives and relationships with friends, in that they were too ashamed to have friends round:

> *It's just too embarrassing, I'd never have people back here. It's just too awful.* (15-year-old female, south coast)

Further details about this issue are included in Chapter 4.

Two additional factors were mentioned very frequently by the young people, when they were talking about their homes. The first was the difficulty caused by not having enough bedrooms in the house, in particular having to share a bedroom with a sibling, and sometimes other relatives. One third of the young people said that they had to share a bedroom with at least one brother or sister, and several with two or three of their siblings. A number of the families had three children in one bedroom, and two of the families had eight children in two bedrooms.

Five households had to use the lounge for sleeping in as there was not enough room for everyone in the family to sleep in a bedroom. Each of the young people affected found it very difficult:

> It's difficult. There's nowhere, like, to be on your own. I go out in the garden sometimes, in the rain, just to be on my own, to get some peace. There's nowhere else to go. (15-year-old male, south coast)

The young people who were living in hotel and bed and breakfast accommodation said that not having their own room or any privacy was particularly difficult. One of the young men, for example, who was living in temporary accommodation in a hotel, said that they had three children in one room, with his parents and a younger sibling in a room down the corridor. There was no lounge in the hotel, so their bedrooms were used to cook, eat and sleep in.

The effects of lack of space and privacy on family relationships are described further in Chapter 5. The figures given here regarding the young people's accommodation clearly demonstrate the difficulties faced by these young people, particularly in comparison to other young people their age. A recent national survey, for example, found that 80 per cent of 13- to 16-year-olds have homes with three or more bedrooms (Balding, 1996). Very few of the young people in this study had that many rooms, despite the fact that many had large families.

There was evidence that not having enough room to live in became much more problematic with age. Sharing a room was particularly difficult for some of the older teenagers in the study, the 15- to 18-year-olds, who felt that having a space of their own was something that young people their age should have. All the young people who shared said that it was a problem for them in some way – it affected their privacy, meant that they were never able to be alone, and invariably caused disagreements and arguments. As one young person, who had recently moved with his family from a home of their own to a bed and breakfast, said:

At the time I wasn't very happy...changing from your own privacy to letting other people know your business...it's a kind of place where you've got to live with other people, so obviously you lose some of your independence. (15-year-old male, south coast, bed and breakfast)

Many of the 15- to 18-year-olds in the study made comments about lack of space. 'You need more privacy at this age, more time to be on your own', as one 16-year-old put it.

For many of the young people, not having their own bedroom, or not having a lounge, was compounded by their low or non-existent income, as it meant that they could not afford to socialise outside the home. Many added that this was particularly difficult in the winter months.

The second issue that emerged for many of the young people in the study, in relation to their accommodation, was the area that they lived in. These comments were most common amongst the young people living in the west of England and Scotland. The young people often said that, although the house or flat they lived in was 'fine' or 'not too bad', the area they lived in was dangerous or unpleasant. Several of these young people also felt that the area they lived in directly affected their chance of getting a job, or affected how people reacted to them:

But when they find out you live in [this area], it's 'stay away from here' and you're out of the door. (18-year-old female, Scotland)

No one wants you once they know you're from round here. (16-year-old male, south coast)

The way in which the area they lived in affected the young people's lives and future prospects is also explored in Chapters 7 and 8.

PARENTS' EMPLOYMENT HISTORY AND INCOME

The majority of the young people in the study said that their parents had not worked for some considerable time. In response to the question about how long their parents had been out of work and on benefits, three-quarters of the responses were as follows:

They've not worked since I was born. (14-year-old male, south coast)

I can't ever remember her working. (17-year-old female, west of England)

> *He's never worked, we've always been on benefits, as long as I can remember.* (16-year-old female, south coast)

This was particularly so in relation to the mothers in the study, many of whom had never worked while their children were growing up. Eight of the parents were out of work because of serious illness or injury that had occurred in the last few years. The remainder of the parents had been out of work for between one and three years.

The majority of the young people did not have any idea, or very much idea, about how much money their family had coming into the house. Forty-two of the young people responded to the question about amount and types of benefit as follows:

> *Don't know, don't ask.* (16-year-old male, Scotland)

> *Not much, just benefits, the dole and child allowance like.* (16-year-old female, west of England)

> *Well, my mum has books, two books I think, and she gets money for them but I don't know how much.* (13-year-old female, south coast)

The remaining 18 young people said that they did know how much money was coming in to their family from benefits, and other sources. There was no pattern to those who said that they knew how much money their family had coming in, by age or location. These figures ranged from £50 to £180 a week, with the average being £95. Those young people who said they knew how much was coming were generally able to detail this, such as £18 child allowance and £76 income support.

In talking about the income that their family had, a large number of the young people also made comments about how little they thought it was:

> *It's £70 a week from the social, but that's nothing, it really isn't.* (14-year-old male, south coast)

> *It's not much, it's really hard for mum to manage with all of us on that.* (15-year-old female, west of England)

> *Eighty quid for them to look after the two of us, it's nothin', just not enough.* (16-year-old male, south coast)

The young people's views about how their family managed on the income they had are discussed later, in Chapters 3 and 5.

Finally in this section, the young people were asked whether their parents had any other sources of income apart from their benefits. For the majority – 42 families – the young people did not think that their parents had any other money coming into the home apart from benefits. For the remaining 18, the young people did identify other sources of income. These were mainly where parents were working occasionally or for a few hours a week, such as doing cleaning or working as a lollipop lady; a few parents were involved in more systematic work, such as working every day in a pub. Four of the families had additional income, on a regular basis, from other relatives or a boyfriend/girlfriend.

The majority of the young people whose parents were doing additional work did not see this as problematic or wrong, and did not seem concerned in talking about it:

> *You can't blame her, can you? She spends all the money she gets from the social on us...the money she earns is just for bits and pieces for herself.* (15-year-old female, west of England)

> *No she's not meant to, but it's difficult to live on benefits so she needs to do other work too.* (16-year-old male, south coast)

> *Everyone does it don't they, why shouldn't he?* (17-year-old female, west of England)

Others were more circumspect, believing that their parents would get into trouble if it became known they were working while signing on:

> *No one will know my name will they? I mean it's not legal is it, but she can't manage otherwise, she doesn't have a choice.* (14-year-old female, south coast)

> *He does work yeah, I hope he doesnae get caught, then he'd have tae pay it all back wouldn't they?* (16-year-old male, Scotland)

Many added that they were very anxious about what would happen if their parents were 'caught out', and were always having to be careful about what they said about where their parents were or what they were doing: 'I don't mention it to anyone, no one,' one 14-year-old young woman said, 'you learn to be careful, mind what you say'.

CHAPTER 3

The young people's income

SIZE OF YOUNG PEOPLE'S INCOME

The young people's own income, like that of their families more broadly, varied greatly. The sample was asked about their income, and where they got their money from. As the income of most young people varied over time, they were asked to give as an example the amount of money they had coming in during the previous week.

The size of the young people's weekly income is shown in Table 2.

Table 2 *The young people's weekly income*

Amount	Number
No income	6
£1–£10 a week	30
£30 plus	14
Did not say/ no information	10

As it shows, six of the young people (10 per cent of the whole group) said that they had no income at all in the previous week. These young people were all aged 15, 16 or 17, and were not in education, training or work. They included a number of young people who were of school age, but who were excluded from school, or who were not attending (see Chapter 7 for further information about these young people).

Another 30 young people had £10 or less to spend in the previous week. These figures were particularly prevalent amongst those who were in the younger age range, the 13- and 14-year-olds. Fourteen of the young people had over £30 to spend in the previous week. Of this group, four were receiving grants for education and training, two were receiving benefits including severe hardship allowance, and seven had a part-time job. There was also evidence that eight young people in the study received regular income from some form of illegal activity, including shoplifting, theft and burglary (which is discussed further in Chapter 8). The Scottish young people reported some of the highest incomes for the previous week.

As demonstrated above, the young people's income varied greatly according to their age and current status. Not surprisingly, it was the older groups in the study who had the highest incomes, often receiving small grants for education and training, whilst others had part-time work. Many of the young people in the study had no income at all, generally because their parents could not afford to give them pocket money, and/or because they could not get any part-time work. It is of note that over half of the sample had between £1 and £10 to spend in the previous week. This is less than national averages – a large national study undertaken by the University of Exeter, for example, found that young people's total weekly incomes average approximately £10.50 (Balding, 1996).

Despite the variations in income shown in Table 2, these figures should not necessarily be taken at face value. Many of the young people gave whatever income they had to their parents, or contributed a large proportion of their income to cover the families' bills. This is an important issue, which is discussed again later in this chapter.

It was clear that very few of the young people had any savings, and also that few had any debts. Most managed, often with a great deal of difficulty, on the money that they had coming in. In total seven young people had savings of up to £20; eight young people had savings of between £20 and £200. There was little evidence that this was age-related, with young people of different ages often having very similar amounts of savings. It is worth noting that many of those with the largest amount of savings said that they were saving up for the future, in particular for further or higher education, or for any emergencies that they or their families might have.

Only five of the young people said that they had any debts. These ranged from £10 up to £200, and were mainly for credit card bills (in friends' names), and debts to parents or to grandparents. A number of young people commented on the need to avoid getting into debt when you are on a low income:

> *It's serious, you have to avoid it. I borrowed £20 from my brother-in-law at Christmas and I'm still paying it off. You think 'Oh it's OK I'll pay it off really quick' but it's hard, you just don't have the money spare.* (15-year-old female, south coast)

Many of the young people added that they were trying desperately hard to manage on the money they had, and were always well aware of when the next lot of money would be coming in.

The things that the young people said that they spent their money on did not distinguish them from any other group of young people (see Balding, 1996). The same things came up repeatedly – sweets, CDs, tapes, cigarettes, clothes, magazines, snacks, bus fares, 'going out', take-away food, make-up, and jewellery. A small number of young people spent most of their money on illegal drugs, which will be considered further in Chapter 6.

CONTRIBUTION TO FAMILY INCOME

Finally, the young people were asked about whether they gave any of their income to their family, to contribute towards household bills or food. Two-thirds of the sample (40 young people) said that they did not do this, although many of this group said that this was because they did not have any money, or only had a very small income. Others said that when they did have any income (such as when they were working) they did give money to their parents. Those who did give their parents some money generally gave variable amounts, depending on what they had, and what the financial situation of their parents was.

The statistics above, however, do not tell the whole story. A number of the young people paid off any large household bills that came in, using their own money and savings, or did extra work where possible so they could pay more to their family or when their parents were struggling. Some of the young people's comments reflect this:

> *If my mum's toughed up for money I go and buy the milk and her bread [using own money] and I go up to Safeways and buy her vegetables and all.* (14-year-old male, west of England)

Sometimes I give my mum a bit every week in case she's a bit short, and I buy stuff for us. (13-year-old male, south coast, bed and breakfast)

Often mum's just not got anything, so I get whatever I can, use any money I've got saved up to get her stuff. (16-year-old male, west of England)

Another young person effectively gave back the £5 or £6 that he got from his mum as pocket money, so that she could buy food:

I buy [her] stuff from the shops when she needs it...it can add up...sometimes I've no pocket money left. (15-year-old male, west of England)

Many of the young people in this study took responsibility for buying in extra food for the family, and contributing to any large bills. This issue is discussed further in Chapters 5 and 6, and in the thematic analyses in Chapter 10.

A number of the young people talked about the necessity of contributing to the family income because they felt it wasn't just their parents' responsibility to provide for the family. Many of the young people repeatedly mentioned the fact that their parents were on a very low income, and that they all had to work together in order to get by. As one young man said:

[I give money to mum when she's short]...It's only fair that. We're a family and we have to bind together. (15-year-old male, south coast, bed and breakfast)

Another added that

It's hard for them with all of us. We have to help out with money, and by not asking for stuff. (14-year-old male, south coast)

The issue of responsibility and roles within the family is an important one, and will be returned to later in the report.

ISSUES AROUND INCOME AND SPENDING

A number of other important issues came out of the discussions with young people about their income. First, it was clear that many of the young people had fluid amounts of income, doing occasional work, getting money from their family, or getting money from illegal activities. Asking the young people about their income the previous week was a useful indicator of income (a snapshot essentially) but was clearly not giving a fully accurate picture of the young people's income. Future research studies in this area might well be advised to use diaries, completed over several months, to record this information properly.

Second, as demonstrated above, it was clear that the sample had access to different sources of income. Those with a part-time job, who were generally in the 15–18 age group, had more money and were more able to do the things that they wanted to do, as well as contribute to the family income. Many of those who did not have a part-time job, particularly those at school, were keen to get one for this reason. However, it was also clear that there was an area effect here, with most part-time work available for the south coast sample, and much less part-time work available in the west of England and in Scotland. The young people in Scotland were also more likely than those in the other two areas to get money through such things as occasional work and illegal activities.

Third, it was also clear that the money that was given to the young people by their parents was meant to cover most (or all) of the expenses that the young people had, including transport, money for lunch at school, food in the day, etc. It was also evident that pocket money was being paid in a different way for most of this group, particularly the under 16s, than it would be in more affluent populations. In many of the families in this study, pocket money was often only given when the parents could afford it. It was rarely seen as a right, and something that should increase with age. There was a general acceptance amongst most of the young people who received money from their parents that they were being given the most that could be afforded. Indeed, some of the young people said that they had agreed to have less (or no) money from their parents, as a way of contributing something to the family income. This is reflected in the following comment:

> It's not that they're mean, they just can't afford it for me and my little sister and my little brother. So I don't get any, like, as my bit towards bills and food and stuff. (13-year-old female, south coast)

This was further demonstrated by the fact that many of the young people with part-time jobs said that they did not receive any money from their parents once they got a Saturday or part-time job. Several young people mentioned that this allowed the family's money to go further, or for pocket money to be able to be paid to younger siblings.

Fourth, a number of families did not deal in money at all, but rather exchanged resources between the parents and their children in kind. For example, a number of those young people with no income said that their parents provided food or cigarettes for them; another was paying for driving lessons for her son. Others shared things between them when one person had them – this was particularly the case for cigarettes (which is discussed further in Chapter 6).

Finally, in this section of the interview the young people were asked whether they felt that there was anything that a young person their age should have, that they couldn't afford to have. Most of the young people named something here, such as smart clothes, games, CDs, a bike, trainers, hi-fi, or a computer, reflecting the answers that might be given to this question by any group of young people. Only six of the young people said that they didn't need anything, that they had what they wanted.

It is of note, however, that many of the young people added a comment in response to this question. This was that these were things that they wanted rather than things that they needed or should have. For example, as one young person said:

Well there's lots of things that I'd like, but no, nothing that I need. (14-year-old male, south coast)

Other comments from the young people reflected this viewpoint:

I've got a computer, I've got games, I've got clothes, I don't need anything else. (13-year-old male, south coast, bed and breakfast)

Obviously I'd like lots of money to do things, but you can't have everything. (16-year-old female, west of England)

I've got everything that I would want. I have got enough. I just take what my ma and da give me and I don't say anything about it, I'm happy with what I've got. (16-year-old female, Scotland)

As long as I've got love off my parents, and support...that's more important than radios and things like that. (13-year-old female, south coast)

I've got what the average 13-year-old has got. (13-year-old male, west of England)

Despite this, the frustration of feeling you have much less money than many other people did come through in some of the young people's comments:

[I would like] the freedom to just be able to say on the spot that you can do things. (17-year-old female, south coast)

The issue of money and spending recurs in the chapters that follow. In particular, the issue of income was central to the young people's social lives, notably how often they were able to see their friends, and what they did in their spare time. This is explored in the next chapter.

CHAPTER 4

Friends and social lives

T he young people in the study were asked about their friends, and what they did socially. In particular, the focus was on whether the young people thought that the limited income that they and their family had affected their social lives and their leisure activities.

FRIENDS

The majority of the young people said that their friends lived in the immediate area near their home. A number of factors, however, affected how often a small number of the sample were able to see their friends. Two of the young people living in bed and breakfast accommodation had been moved 40 miles away from their home, and hence had left most of their friends behind. Both said they had not been able to make new friends, and were as a result hoping to move back to their previous home area at some point.

Six young people, mostly those living in the west of England, lived in isolated, rural areas, and found seeing their friends regularly a problem. This was primarily because of lack of money for transport either to visit their friends, or to meet them in the nearest town. This problem was compounded by the fact that most of the parents or relatives of this group did not have a car, and so could not help them with transport. The additional factor which affected six young people's social lives was that they had no telephone in their homes, which led to a feeling of isolation and difficulty in arranging social events:

> You really feel cut off, can't speak to your mates, and people don't contact me now 'cause it's too difficult, they'd have to call in.
> (15-year-old male, south coast, bed and breakfast)

It was clear also that some young people felt restricted in their social activities by local gang activities and rivalries. This was particularly so for many of the Scottish young people in the study, who commented that they lived in 'rough' and poor areas of town where gang violence and rivalry was common.

LEISURE ACTIVITIES

A minority of the sample (20 young people) believed that their income did not affect the leisure activities they were able to participate in. The interviews showed, however, that most of the young people believed that their limited income did affect the leisure activities they could participate in, and their social lives. The third of the sample who said their income didn't affect their social lives said things like:

I'm quite happy with what I'm doing. I would not change my routine, I like what I do. (16-year-old female, Scotland)

No it doesn't, not really. I just put up with the things I can do and accept the things I can't do. (15-year-old male, south coast)

However, as is clear in the response of this last young person, many of this group were accepting their situation as it was, and had in many ways got used to living a 'restricted' lifestyle. The underlying message seemed to be that they would rather have the money to do other things, but have accepted that they do not. Also, a few of the young people had settled into a routine which they did not imagine was ever likely to change, mainly because of the limited opportunities available in their area. There was thus a sense that many of the young people were 'putting up with' the inevitable. It was clear, in fact, that their limited income did affect most young people's leisure activities, social lives, and sense of purpose. For example:

We don't do nothing, nothing in particular...sit in the close and have a drink. (17-year-old female, Scotland)

You just get pissed off doing the same things, gets on your nerves just staying in most of the week...[most days I]...get stoned, sit on my arse, play the computer, stay in, and that's it till the next day, just get up and get stoned again. (16-year-old male, Scotland)

Listen to music, take the dog out. It's just the same, you get used to it, not doing anything. (16-year-old male, south coast)

[What do you do in the evenings?]
Nothing, just walk the street or sit in the Close...if we've got the spare money we go in the community centre and have a cup of tea or something or a packet of crisps, like we sit in there and that passes the time.
[Do you feel that the evenings are long?]
Sometimes, aye. (14-year-old female, Scotland)

The remaining 40 young people made a number of comments about how their own and their family's income affected their friendships and their social lives. Many of the young people named the leisure activities that they were not able to participate in because of not having enough money. The two things most often mentioned were (i) going to the cinema, and (ii) a range of sports including swimming, cycling, basketball, gymnastics, ice skating, rugby, keep fit, cricket, go-karting, and badminton. Most pointed out that it was not simply the cost of doing the activity, but the costs of travelling to where it was held, hiring equipment etc. One young person, for example, had always wanted to go with his friends to one of the sports clubs run in his area over the summer:

They cost £20 or £25 and I can't afford it 'cause like we've done shopping beforehand or something. (13-year-old male, south coast)

A number of young people commented on how, over the years, they had become used to thinking that they would not ever be able to do organised activities. Most did not ever anticipate having enough money to be able to do even the most basic things.

Other young people talked not so much about the individual activities that they couldn't get involved in because of their limited income, but how it affected their friendships and their family relationships:

We can't afford to all go out together, as a family, like to the pictures, it's just too expensive. (14-year-old male, south coast)

The effects of a limited income on family relationships are explored in the next chapter. Not being able to participate in organised activities, and the boredom that resulted from this, also led several young people to get involved in vandalism and crime (see Chapter 8).

CHAPTER 5

Family relationships

T his chapter explores the family circumstances and family relationships of the young people, focusing on the effects of a limited income on the young people's relationships with their family.

FAMILY COMPOSITION

The living circumstances of the sample are shown in Table 3. As the table shows, 31 young people lived with two people. Of this group, 15 lived with both their natural parents, and 16 young people lived in a step-family, with one natural parent and his/her partner. Of the remainder, 27 young people lived in a single-parent family, all except one of whom was headed by a mother. One young person was living with an elder sister, as his mother had recently died. These figures do not reflect national statistics. A recent large-scale study found that, for 13- to 16-year-olds, 70 per cent lived with both natural parents, 15 per cent with a single parent, and 10 per cent in a step-family (Balding, 1996). There

Table 3 *Family composition of the sample*

Living with...	Number
Both natural parents	15
One natural parent and a step-parent/partner	16
Lone parent	27
Older sister	1
Unclear	1

was thus a greater number of young people in this study living in step-families and single-parent families. The higher proportion of single-parent families living in poverty has been well documented (Kumar, 1993; Dennehy *et al.*, 1997), a fact clearly reflected in this study.

There was a high proportion of young people in this study who had no contact with at least one birth parent, generally their natural father. In total, 34 of the young people said that they *did* have contact with both birth parents, although five described their relationship with their father as 'practically non-existent' or very strained. Those who said that they had contact with only one birth parent accounted for just over one third of the sample, 23 young people. For five of this group this was because of the death of the parent; for the remainder they had 'lost touch over time', never knew who their other parent was, or did not have contact because of that person's violence within the family.

The fluidity of family life for many of the young people in this study needs to be noted. Many of the young people described major changes that had taken place in their families over the past few years. This was particularly so for those who, in Table 3, were described as living in step-families or lone-parent families, who had often experienced a number of changes in family composition during their lifetime.

Family relationships

The young people were asked about their relationship with their parents. It was clear from their comments that relationships with mothers were generally rated as better than relationships with fathers (or step-fathers where applicable). This reflects the findings of research, such as that by Catan *et al.* (1996). It is of note that there were no differences here in relationships between step-parents and natural parents.

When asked about their relationship with their mothers, over half the sample – 32 young people – described this as 'very good', with 26 young people describing it as 'OK/average', and two as 'not very good'. The young people gave a wide variety of reasons for describing their relationship with their mothers in these ways. Those who described it as 'very good' often said that this was because they 'don't argue' or because 'we just get on well'. In general, these young people talked about the supportive aspects of their relationship with their mothers. For example:

I just get along with her really good. (17-year-old male, west of England)

Because there is only me and my ma and I have only got my ma to talk to...I tell my ma everything. (13-year-old female, Scotland)

She's always there for me and she just like...listens to me...I just tell my mum everything. (13-year-old female, south coast)

We're more like friends than mother and daughter. (15-year-old female, west of England)

She is always there to support me. (16-year-old female, Scotland)

We talk to each other. If I have a problem we make sure it's sorted out there and then, it's not carried over and bottled up. (17-year-old female, west of England)

A few young people described their relationship with their mother as 'very good' for more practical reasons, for example:

Well she gives me money, that's it really. (13-year-old female, west of England)

Another young person described his relationship with his mother as very good because she 'does everything' for him around the house, such as washing his clothes and cooking.

It was clear, however, that the vast majority of this group of young people described the supportive and close relationship that they had with their mother in the ways illustrated above. This was particularly so in the case of those mothers who were single parents – many of the young people commented on how their mother had had to bring them and their siblings up single handed. As has already been demonstrated in relation to household finances, many of the young people in single-parent families in particular recognised the difficulties their parent faced in bringing them up, and many reflected on this fact when describing their relationship with them.

Those young people who described their relationship with their mother as 'average' or 'not very good' generally said it was because they argued with their mum, or because she wouldn't let them do things they wanted to do. Most often mentioned were not being allowed to stay out late at night, and arguments about untidy bedrooms or helping around the house.

Relationships with fathers were much more variable and not always as positive as those with mothers. Only 16 of the young people described their relationship with their father (or stepfather) as 'very good', with 21 saying it was 'OK' or 'average', and 4 as 'not very good'. It needs to be remembered in this context that, as detailed above, a significant proportion of the sample did not have contact with their fathers, either because of death, divorce, or never having known them. Those who described their relationship with their father as very good explained this in a number of ways, including that they spent time together and did things together.

[It's very good because] I help him out, and he helps me out, and we spend a lot of our time together. (13-year-old male, west of England)

Or it was because of how they perceived their father's attitude towards them:

My dad just likes me a lot. (16-year-old male, west of England)

I get everything I want. I ask for it and he gets me it. (15-year-old female, Scotland)

He just lets me do anything. (14-year-old female, west of England)

It was notable that the young people from Asian or Middle Eastern families in the study were particularly positive towards their fathers. Most described the importance of respecting and valuing fathers in their culture. As one young person, whose family was originally from the Middle East, described it:

I respect him, and he has worked very hard to bring up me and my sister. In my culture it is very important to respect your father. (17-year-old male, south coast)

Those young people who described their relationship with their father as 'OK'/'average', or 'not very good', did so because of problems or difficulties with their relationship. These included in four cases their father's violent behaviour or alcoholism, and in five cases lack of contact and cancellation of promised visits. For others it was because 'we argue a lot', and that he didn't let them do things that they wanted to do, such as staying out late.

CAUSES OF CONFLICT

One of the things that is clear from the results of this chapter so far is that very few of the young people mentioned that their relationship with their parents was affected by the family's limited income. This finding was further demonstrated by the results of a question about what their family argued or disagreed about most often. Three areas were most commonly the cause of arguments. First, one-third (20) of the young people said they mainly argued with family members about household tasks and untidiness in the house. Second, 20 young people said that they argued mainly over possessions, in particular clothes and the use of the television. Third, 18 young people said that their family mainly argued about going out, and the time they had to be in at night.

Only three of the young people said explicitly that they argued with their parents about money:

Money is our biggest problem, it's the thing we argue about. (17-year-old female, west of England)

[We argue when] I forget how little she has or I get frustrated by it. (16-year-old male, south coast)

However, although only three young people named money as a source of conflict in the family, it is clear that it affected family relationships in a broad range of often more subtle ways. These are demonstrated in detail in other chapters and in Theme 3 (p. 61), and included younger siblings not understanding the real impact of their family's low income, disputes over space and attempts to get some privacy, and not being able to do activities together as a family because of the cost. It is of note, however, that even when they argued over money, some of the young people had to think about the financial implications of having an argument:

I've stormed out of the house but I would never chuck anything in my house because it would just break things and cost money at the end of the day, and we just can't afford it. (15-year-old male, west of England)

Parents' aspirations for their children

It was clear that the parents' concerns about the difficult financial circumstances they were living in greatly affected what they wanted for their children in the future. In response to the question about what they thought their parents wanted for them in the future, the young people's views fell into three main categories. First, 35 young people said that their parents often talked about concrete things that they wanted for them in the future, for example to do well at school and get a good job:

Just to get a job and things like that. (13-year-old female, south coast)

Just get a job. (16-year-old male, Scotland)

To have a good job and get a good place to live. (15-year-old female, west of England)

To be healthy and have a good family, and have a lot of food and good surroundings. (13-year-old male, Scotland)

To be happily married...to be well off, not poor, have a nice house and a nice family. (15-year-old female, west of England)

Second, a smaller group of young people (14) said that their parents often talked about wanting them to get out of or stay out of trouble with the law. This was generally in relation to those who were already in trouble in some way, or who had a history of being involved in crime and illegal activities. These comments were most often made by the young men in the study. For example:

For me to keep out of trouble...get a job. (16-year-old male, west of England)

Just to keep out of trouble with the law. (17-year-old male, west of England)

To not go to prison, to go straight. (18-year-old male, south coast)

The criminal activities of this group are discussed further in Chapter 8.

Third, the most common comment was that the young people thought their parents wanted them to do better than they had. In particular the young people described how their parents wanted them to avoid the mistakes that they had made, and to live a more comfortable life than their family was at present. Two-thirds of the sample (40 young people) mentioned this as something that their parents wanted for them. For example:

> *They don't wanna see me in the same situation as them.* (17-year-old female, west of England)

> *She doesn't want me to turn out like she has.* (13-year-old female, south coast)

> *To continue my education and not end up the way that they have.* (15-year-old male, south coast)

> *To have more choice than she had.* (17-year-old female, south coast)

> *She wants me to do well and not make the same mistakes she did.* (15-year-old female, west of England)

> *To get a good job so that if I get made unemployed like he did then I'll be able to get another job. He wants me to do better than he's done.* (14-year-old male, south coast)

> *Just to get on and have more money than they did, not be unemployed like them.* (13-year-old female, west of England)

The parents' influence on the young people's own aims and aspirations is considered again in Chapters 7 and 9.

CHAPTER 6

Physical health

YOUNG PEOPLE'S VIEW OF THEIR PHYSICAL HEALTH

The young people were asked a range of questions about their physical health. To introduce the topic, they were asked whether they felt their health was 'very good', 'average/OK' or 'not very good'. The majority of the sample – 43 young people – said that their health was average or OK. Of the remainder, 13 described their health as very good, and three as not very good.

There were a number of reasons why the young people described their health in this way. Those who viewed it as very good generally said that this was because they were 'never ill', that they had 'not had any problems', and that they were 'very fit and healthy'. Those who said their health had not been very good or that it had been poor said that this was because they had had a serious illness such as glandular fever, or that they were 'completely unfit' or overweight.

As stated above, however, the majority of the young people said that their health over the last year had been average or OK. The reasons the young people gave for this were very varied, and included the following:

- 'quite fit but not very fit'

- has bad asthma

- 'had loads of colds and flu'

- has broken several bones in last year

- 'because I'm overweight, like heavy'

- 'I feel OK but not very healthy'

- 'I smoke a lot and that makes my chest feel bad'

- 'I don't eat very well and I'm not very healthy'

The range of responses under this heading demonstrates the many different definitions and perceptions of 'health' and 'healthy' amongst the young people. This is an important issue, with implications for health education (for a discussion see Brannen *et al.*, 1994). Some young people interpreted 'healthy' as meaning 'how you feel now, today', and said they found it difficult to think about the implications of what they did now for their health in the future.

ACCESS TO GPS

The young people were then asked about whether they had any difficulty getting access to a GP, or getting advice and information about their health when they wanted it. There was a universal response on this question – that the young people did not have any difficulty getting to a GP, or getting health information. The only additional comments made were as follows: three people (mainly those in the west of England sample who lived in rural areas) said that their GP surgery was some distance away and not on a bus route, which meant that they had to walk. Two more said that it was a long (and expensive) bus journey to their GPs. Two said they often had to wait two days (or more) for an appointment, by which time the problem had either got worse or gone away. Three individuals (all in the south coast sample and in temporary accommodation) said how difficult it was to make contact with their GP or other agencies when they didn't have a telephone in their home:

When you're feeling bad the last thing you wanna do is go and hang around a phone box in the rain. (15-year-old male, south coast, bed and breakfast)

DENTAL HEALTH

The young people's view of their dental health was more varied than their view about their physical health. Only 12 young people said they would describe their dental health as 'good' or 'very good', with 26 saying it was 'OK' or average, and 22 saying that it was 'not very good'. The young people who did not think that their teeth were very good generally said that they had had a number of problems with them, including cracked teeth, missing teeth, a lot of fillings, bleeding gums, and painful teeth. Many of the young people added that they had not been to the dentist in the last year or so, because of fear, not getting round to it, and thinking they'll be told off/criticised. None of the young people mentioned the cost or any charges as a reason for them not going. Five young people mentioned that they visited the dentist regularly in order to avoid developing any problems in the future, that might then be expensive to have treated.

FOOD AND NUTRITION

The next part of the interview asked the young people about the food that they ate, and whether they felt that their family's limited income affected the type or quantity of food that they had. A majority of the sample – 40 young people – believed that their family's income did not affect what they ate. For example:

There's always a lot of stuff, none of us ever goes hungry. (13-year-old female, south coast)

We eat very well. (13-year-old male, west of England)

Mum goes a bit over the top with the shopping. (15-year-old female, south coast)

We've always got food in the cupboards. (15-year-old male, west of England)

Well we can't go to Marks and Spencers seven days a week, but it's fine, we've got no problems with it. (15-year-old male, south coast)

[Mum spends a lot on food]...she says we're growing and it's important to have a lot of food. (13-year-old male, south coast)

There's always plenty of food for us. (17-year-old female, south coast)

This suggests, therefore, that the majority of the young people did not feel that their families' low income affected the food that they ate.

There was also evidence, however, that some parents were spending less on themselves, in order to ensure that there was enough food available. For example, one young man described how his mother 'never buys stuff for her alone', in order to get sufficient food in instead. Another said that

> *[Mum] struggles for money, she disnae buy herself nothing, just spends it on food.* (14-year-old male, Scotland)

Parents (and in particular mothers) sacrificing their own needs for their children has been demonstrated in a number of other studies (Kumar, 1993; Barnardos, 1995; Kempson, 1996).

As shown in Chapter 3, some of the young people were themselves contributing their pocket money or earnings from a part-time job in order to keep sufficient food in the house. Many of the young people who said that the family's income did not affect what they ate, said that they did not think of their own contribution as linked to this.

The remaining group – 20 young people – believed that the limited income their family had coming in did affect the amount and type of food that they could buy. The effects were seen not so much in terms of quantity of food, but in terms of what sort of food was bought, and when. The following examples were given:

- buying a lot of mince meat as it was cheaper during the BSE scare;

- having chips with every meal because they are cheap and filling;

- seeing mum borrow money from friends or neighbours when food supplies were running low;

- not being able to ask friends to their home for a meal because there wasn't enough food to go round;

- always having fry-ups because they're cheap;

- always having cheap but filling foods, such as pasta, potatoes, bread;

- if a large bill came in at the beginning of the week, having to stretch food out to last the rest of the week;

- always having to eat their family's traditional food – Middle Eastern food – because it was cheaper, rather than because they wanted to;

- having sandwiches for every meal towards the end of the week, because they are cheap;

- running out of food at the end of the week;

- not being able to afford 'proper' food, such as meat and fish;

- always having to buy reduced foods, or those near their sell-by dates;

- always having to have 'the same old cheap and boring foods' for every meal, such as beans, chips, and bread.

These factors are reflected in the young people's comments below:

Mum's most worried about food. (16-year-old male, west of England)

My sister works at Sainsbury's at the weekend and we go to the staff shop for reduced stuff. Like 10p stuff, 10p ham, so we have reduced meats, freeze it down. Like 5p bread. (15-year-old female, west of England)

All the cupboards used to be jam-packed when dad was working but now there often isn't that much food. (16-year-old male, south coast)

Some weeks if we've not got any money...we just don't get as much. (17-year-old male, Scotland)

Sometimes when it's that bad we very rarely have enough meals to last us a week. (13-year-old male, south coast)

We always have to buy reduced stuff. (15-year-old female, west of England)

[We can't always afford a breakfast]...ma cannae afford to go out and buy bacon and all that every day. (17-year-old female, Scotland)

Sometimes you just want something a bit different and we haven't got money for that. (15-year-old female, south coast)

[Mum] has not got enough to buy, like, dear food and that. (13-year-old female, Scotland)

It therefore became clear in many of the young people's responses to these questions that, although initially they said that their income had little or no effect on what they ate, further questioning showed that it was often in fact a key issue.

Smoking, alcohol and drugs

The final set of questions in the physical health section of the interview asked the young people about their cigarette use, and their consumption of alcohol and illegal drugs.

First, in terms of smoking, just over half of the sample (34 young people) did not smoke. Thus 26 of the sample were smokers, which is a slightly greater proportion than figures for the national adolescent population (Coleman, 1997). More smokers were found in the Scottish and west of England areas than amongst the south coast young people. It was equally common amongst the males and females in the sample. The young people who smoked had generally started at a young age, usually 11 or 12, and said that they had either been encouraged to try a cigarette by a friend, or wanted to fit in with their peer group. Those who did smoke smoked between 10 and 75 cigarettes a week, with the average being 50 a week.

It is of note also that a larger number – 48 of the 60 young people in the sample – lived in a home where someone smoked; 17 young people lived with two or more smokers. Again, this is much higher than in the general population – statistics for 16-year-olds show that 35 per cent have a parent who smokes (Balding, 1996). This same survey showed that half of the 11- to 16-year-olds lived in a home where at least one person smoked. Cigarettes were also a key commodity for many of the smokers – cigarettes were often negotiated as payment for casual work, or were given in lieu of pocket money.

Second, in terms of alcohol use, half of the sample (31 young people) did not use alcohol. These young people were mainly in the younger age group involved in the study, the 13- and 14-year-olds. Of the remaining 29 young people who said they did drink alcohol, 14 drank 'occasionally', generally once a week or a few times a month. The others were more regular drinkers, generally saying they drank 'a couple of pints a day', 'most nights', or 'three cans a night'. The young people in the south coast sample drank the least amount of alcohol; the young people in Scotland drank the most. Several of the young people described how alcohol relieved the boredom and frustration of their lives (a theme further explored in Chapter 9).

Third, a number of the young people in the study had occasionally or regularly used illegal drugs. Those who had never tried illegal drugs represented almost two-thirds of the sample, 38 young people. Seven young people had used an illegal drug, usually cannabis, just once or very rarely, or only took them a few times a year. Those who were regular users of illegal drugs accounted for 15 young people, the majority of whom were in the Scottish sample. These young people described themselves as regular users of illegal drugs, often using them most days or 'whenever I can afford them'.

The drugs most commonly used by the young people were cannabis, speed and ecstasy. Many of the young people who did use illegal drugs said that they would use more of them if they had more money to buy them with. It is of note that some of the young people described how it was sometimes easier to get drugs than alcohol when you didn't have much money. Drugs dealers locally had adjusted to the fact that many people only got money at certain times of the week:

> We can get tickies. We know a lot of dealers so we can go to the dealers and get a tick. They always know we'll pay them back.
> (16-year-old male, Scotland)

> Drugs are different you see, you can go and get them on tick...that means if you've nae got money that's all right, you can give the money when you get paid...you cannae do that wi' alcohol. (17-year-old female, Scotland)

Many of the young people, in their responses to the questions on use of cigarettes, alcohol and illegal drugs, added additional comments about the role of these substances in their lives. One 14-year-old described cigarettes as 'my only pleasure, like that makes me feel good'. Another 15-year-old described alcohol as

> Something to do, get you out of it, forget you've got no money and that there's nothing round here to do. (15-year-old male, west of England)

This is an important issue, which is discussed further in Chapter 10.

School life, current status and future plans

As would be expected with a 13–18 age range, the majority of the young people in the study were at school at the time of the interview. This accounted for 38 young people, almost two-thirds of the sample. In addition, four young people described themselves as 'technically' at school (including two who were registered at special schools), but they were not attending. Four young people (all aged 16–18) were on college courses. The remainder – 14 young people – were in a variety of circumstances but described themselves as 'doing nothing' or 'deciding what to do'. Some of these young people had experienced a year or more of a patchwork of different activities, including short training courses, periods of unemployment, and periods of short-term work. Some members of this group described themselves as 'fighting' with the Benefits Agency to be able to sign on, or get severe hardship payments.

EXPERIENCES OF SCHOOL

The young people's experiences of education were very diverse. Thirty-eight described themselves as 'doing well', 'doing OK' or having 'done well' at school. However, another group (22 young people) said that they had had difficult or unpleasant experiences at school. Many of these young people had not attended school as a result, or had attended two or three schools in a short time; others had been sent to special schools, although some of these attended irregularly. The young people named a variety of problems, including the following:

• difficulties with reading and writing; did not feel he had received sufficient help with this;

- absent because of illness for long periods of time; got behind with school work;

- 'completely and utterly bored';

- bullied by other young people over several years;

- didn't understand the work;

- 'just wasn't interested in it'; it felt completely irrelevant;

- moved to a new school and couldn't make new friends;

- teachers were unpleasant and uncaring;

- 'could not keep up'; found the work too difficult;

- couldn't do the class work or homework; no-one to help her.

A considerable number of the young people in the sample described themselves as taking 'a lot' of time off school. Sixteen young people said they sometimes didn't attend school for days at a time; of these eight young people left school a year before the compulsory school leaving age. Many of these young people had subsequently found it difficult to get work or a place on a training or college course. Several young people described themselves as having 'given up' on ever getting any qualifications. The comments of these young people demonstrate the difficulties they found with school life, and the problems this had subsequently caused them:

If you've got no qualifications like me, they just don't want to know. I get pissed off I really do, with all of it. I don't know what I'm gonna do now. (16-year-old male, south coast)

A number of this group clearly regretted not being able to get more from their school years:

If I'd stayed on at school I might not be here now, I might not be smoking hash. (18-year-old male, Scotland)

I think I missed out on a lot but there's nothing I can do about it now. (15-year-old female, Scotland)

I wish I could go back and do exams. (17-year-old female, Scotland)

The relationship between leaving school early, lack of qualifications, unemployment and (in some cases) offending behaviour has been widely documented (Utting *et al.*, 1993; Audit Commission, 1996; Cullingford and Morrison, 1997). This issue is returned to later, in Chapters 8 and 10.

EFFECT OF FAMILY INCOME ON SCHOOL LIFE

The young people were also asked whether they felt that their family income had affected their school work; whether there was anything that they (had) needed that they couldn't afford; also whether their home situation (such as lack of space) affected their school work. The majority felt that, in fact, their school work had not been greatly affected by these factors. However, 12 individuals did find that it made a difference. These factors included having to ask for discounts for school trips:

> *I used to wait for everybody to go out and then do it.* (15-year-old female, west of England)

> *I had to choose either to have new shoes or go to [the school trip] so I had school shoes instead.* (15-year-old female, west of England)

and not being able to get necessary equipment:

> *Yeah couldn't afford stuff for PE.* (13-year-old male, west of England)

Other young people talked about not being able to buy textbooks, as many better-off young people did when there was a shortage of them at school. Also, several of these young people were told that their school work had to be produced on a word processor, but they didn't have access to one.

FUTURE PLANS

The young people were asked what work they hoped to do in the future, and also how optimistic they were about being able to do this. Only five young people said that they had no idea, or didn't know what work they would like to do in the future. Another four young people said it wouldn't matter what the work was, they just wanted a job and a chance to earn some money. The remaining 51 young people each named a job that they wanted to do. As might be expected, these jobs were very varied, and included shop assistant, doctor, chef, secretary, nursery nurse, plasterer, graphic designer and mechanic.

There were differences, however, in whether they felt that they would be able to do these jobs in the future. Only half of this group – 25 young people – felt that they would be able to get jobs in their preferred field. The remainder said that although they wanted to do a particular job, they did not feel they would ever get the qualifications to enable them to do it:

> *Well yeah I'd like to do design, graphics type work, but...I probably won't get into it, I don't stand a chance really.* (15-year-old male, south coast)

Other research has demonstrated a considerable difference between the numbers of young people who want to, and who think that they will be able to, get a job or pursue a particular career (Balding, 1996). It is worth noting that the most optimistic young people were those who were planning to stay on at school, and who believed that they were doing well at school. The young people on the south coast were the most optimistic that their work ambitions would be fulfilled. The young people's perceptions of the future more broadly are further explored in Chapter 9.

In terms of the young people's views about when they would leave home, the majority were expecting to leave at quite an early age. Thus 30 young people gave the age at which they thought they would leave as 16, 17 or 18. However, many added that this was when they hoped to leave, rather than when they thought they would be able to – most acknowledged the difficulty of doing so, particularly in relation to the costs of renting or buying a place to live. The remaining young people said that they didn't know when they would leave home. At present, the national average age of leaving home is 23. Further, there is evidence that 50 per cent of young men aged 21–24 are still living at home (Coleman, 1997). This issue is further explored in the thematic analyses in Chapter 10.

CHAPTER 8

Crime and the law

O ver half the sample had been involved in breaking the law in some way. Whilst some of these acts had led to involvement with the police, others had not. In total, 33 young people had been (or were) involved in a range of illegal activities. Of this group, 17 young people had been involved in what might be called less serious activities, or had done them some time ago. These activities included, for example, playing with matches and setting light to woodland, graffiti, and some vandalism. The other 16 young people, however, were or had been involved in more serious illegal activities. These included burglary, actual bodily harm, receiving stolen goods, theft, taking and driving away, criminal damage, and arson. These young people were mainly young men.

REASONS FOR INVOLVEMENT IN OR DESISTENCE FROM CRIME

This group of young people had first become involved in these activities in various different ways. Several described the boredom they experienced whilst at school, and how they often got involved in these activities when they were truanting from school:

> *There was just nothing, nothing to do. We just started doing stuff for a laugh really, nothing to do.* (16-year-old male, west of England)

Boredom was also linked to a lack of affordable leisure facilities in the area. Others said that they were friends with a group of older young people who were involved in illegal activities, and that they became drawn in. Most did not talk about being pressured into involvement in crime by their friends, but described how they wanted to keep in with them and not look 'soft':

You need to like, I don't know, it's about being one o' the boys, one o' the lads, not looking chicken. You do things once or twice with them and it's a buzz, there's a real buzz from doing that sort of stuff. (17-year-old male, south coast)

The relationship between involvment in crime and young people's image and representation management has recently been a key focus of research (Emler and Reicher, 1995), and many of the comments of the young people in this study lend weight to the link between the two.

A few of the young people described lack of money as an incentive (or a reason) to get involved in crime. Many described how it was impossible to live on the money that they had, and that they needed to get some extra income in order to survive. Many of this group said that, if they could get a job that paid enough money to live on, they would try to end their illegal activity. Most were well aware of the risks of not doing so, knowing that one day they could end up in prison (see later in this chapter for further discussion of this point).

The majority of the young people who were involved in the more 'serious' criminal activity, described earlier, had been involved with the police; very few said they had been involved in crimes where the police had not been involved. Many of the young people also spoke about their involvement in crime in a very off-hand manner. Few were reticent about talking about the illegal activities they had been involved in, and many (as suggested above) believed it gave them status and a reputation. Several described living in areas where law-breaking was the norm ('everyone's at it round here,' one young man said), most commonly those living in the west of England and Scottish areas. Many described it as hard not to be part of it.

In talking about illegal activities, a few young people said that they had not got involved in crime, because of the impact that it might have on their families' finances:

I know that if I do something [illegal] I would go to court and that'll be a hefty fine, and I know my parents wouldn't be able to pay it because of money problems and things. (15-year-old male, west of England)

Others talked about the impact that crime or a court case might have on their parents' health.

It was clear that many of the young people who were involved in crime also had friends and family members who had been in trouble with the law. Thus 36 of the 60 young people said that their family members or close friends had been involved in crime in some way. Analyses showed that the majority of those involved in the crimes described above were also those who had family members or friends who had been involved in illegal activity. This finding is consistent with that of other studies (Utting *et al.*, 1993). It is interesting in this light that Balding (1996) found similar reasons given by young people for getting into crime as those reported here. In this study, over 40 per cent of offenders said they got involved through family and friends, over 20 per cent because they had no money, and over 10 per cent because they were bored and had nothing to do.

VICTIMS OF CRIME

Finally, the young people were also asked if they had ever been a victim of crime. Over a third of the sample – 22 young people – had been a victim of crime in some way. Of this group, one had been mugged, seven had been attacked or beaten up, one person's family had been victimised and their house smashed up, and 16 had had their homes burgled. Many had experienced two or more of these crimes. National statistics show that those aged 16–29 are one of the most likely groups to be victims of crime (Coleman, 1997), and the results of this study reflect this fact.

It is also worth noting that many of the families in the study did not have house insurance to cover items stolen in house burglaries, so that once things were gone, it was often several months (if ever) before they were replaced.

YOUNG OFFENDERS

In concluding this chapter on young people and crime, it is worth returning to the group of young people who were involved in regular and quite serious crime. This group have already been identified, in Chapter 7, as those who had most commonly:

• had poor experiences of education;

- left school before the minimum leaving age;

- left school with no qualifications;

- had literacy problems;

- had friends and family members who were involved in crime.

Several of this group described a feeling of being 'locked into' law-breaking, saying that it provided them with additional income, enabled them to participate in an activity with friends, gave them a buzz, and relieved the boredom of their daily lives. In talking about their offending, a few believed that they might well end up in prison at some point ('you can't stay lucky forever,' as one young man said). Others were committed to trying to stay out of trouble, but acknowledged that it would be difficult; many of this group talked despondently about their prospects for the future, in particular in relation to getting a job. Without a job to fill their time, and to provide them with an income, many felt that they would continue to be involved in crime, and might well end up in prison as a result.

CHAPTER 9

Living with poverty: now and the future

The last section of the interview asked the young people a range of general questions about their lives. These included their view about their life overall, who they felt close to, what they did when they needed help and advice, how they felt about their circumstances in relation to other people, and whether they thought that living on benefits affected how other people viewed them or treated them.

HOW DO YOU FEEL ABOUT LIFE?

The first part of this section asked the young people how they felt about their lives overall. Just over a third of the sample – 21 young people – described their lives at present in very positive terms, as 'very good', 'excellent' or 'brilliant'. The majority of those answering in this way were from the west of England and south coast samples. Many made comments such as the following:

Yeah it's good, it's really great in fact. (15-year-old female, west of England)

I'm happy, I really like what I've got. (15-year-old female, south coast)

I'm very satisfied, it's really great. My life is satisfactory, happy...I don't need anything really...I'm very happy with my mum and dad. (17-year-old female, west of England)

It's good, I can't believe it...I've got an apprenticeship lined up and a nice girlfriend...yeah really good. (17-year-old male, west of England)

I feel good, very good. I've had some problems and now I'm through them. I've got a good family, we all get on well, and I know my mum loves me. There's not a lot of people can say all that. (13-year-old male, south coast)

It's fine. I'm quite happy with it the way it is. I've got loads of friends...I can do anything I want, school work's fine. (15-year-old male, south coast)

I've got everything that I wanted and there's not really much wrong with me, yeah it's good. (13-year-old male, south coast)'

It's fab, brilliant, fab. (15-year-old female, west of England)

The most common response to this question was that, overall, their life was 'all right' and 'not bad', with 31 young people describing their life in this way. These young people often made qualifying statements, identifying something that would make their lives better. The sorts of responses the young people gave to this question were as follows:

It's fine yeah, I just need to have a bit more money. (15-year-old male, west of England)

It's OK but this is a rough area, there's joyriders up and down the road every night...they keep me awake. (16-year-old female, west of England)

It's OK yeah I'm staying out of trouble. (17-year-old male, west of England)

Five young people described their life overall as 'boring', or said that they 'hated it'. This was because, for example, they had no job or money, or were living a long distance away from friends. For example:

My life is boring, and I'm sorry I haven't helped myself to get more of an education. (17-year-old female, west of England)

I hate it, I hate being here, living here. (17-year-old female, south coast)

I feel bored with my life. I just want to get money and a job and get money...Get my own room. (14-year-old female, Scotland)

This group of young people generally identified all parts of their lives in negative terms, for example not having any friends, money or social life; having a poor relationship with parents; living in poor quality accommodation or in a deprived area.

How do you feel about the future?

The young people were then asked whether they felt positive about their future. It was clear that a greater number of young people were optimistic about the future, compared to the number who felt that their life was going well at present. Thus 31 young people described themselves as being 'very optimistic' about their future; again, however, this represented a greater proportion of the west of England and south coast samples. Those who said that they were very optimistic about the future talked about this in a number of different respects, such as:

I'll get a good job and have a family, start up my own business and then be able to pay my mum, if she gets short of money. (14-year-old male, west of England)

Yeah, at 20 I'll be married with a happy life, pregnant with my first child and a journalist by 28. (15-year-old female, south coast)

As is suggested by these two comments, however, it is not clear how realistic some of these expectations were, and to what extent they were an idealised view of the future. It is also of note that several young people added an 'if' statement to their response on this question, such as their life will be very good 'if I pass my exams', or 'if I get a job'. For example:

If I had a job I would...[feel positive]. (17-year-old male, Scotland)

Yeah I do think it'll be all right, but I've just gotta get into the army. (16-year-old male, south coast)

In total eight young people said that they were 'not at all' optimistic about the future. This was generally said by those who could not get a job, or those who had left school early without any qualifications:

No I'm not optimistic, I mean you just don't know what's going to happen to you...it could totally backfire. (15-year-old female, west of England)

No, not without exams, and I've got none. (16-year-old male, south coast)

Several of these young people were those who were involved in crime, as discussed in Chapter 8.

WHO DO YOU TURN TO?

The second part of this section of the interview asked the young people about people outside the family that they are close to, what they do when they want help or advice, and what things they worry about most often. One question asked the young people whether anyone, apart from their parents, had been helpful or supportive to them while they were growing up. Thirteen young people did not identify anyone who they would describe in this way: for example, 'no, just me and my mum, no one else'. The remaining young people did identify one or more people who had been helpful to them. Aunts, uncles and grand-parents were mentioned by 22 young people, who said for example:

[Grandmother]...when I go up there she's always nice to me...makes me food and listens to me. (17-year-old male, west of England)

[Aunt and uncle]...they're always there if my mum isn't there for me. (15-year-old female, west of England)

Older sisters and brothers were mentioned by seven young people, and sibling's boy- or girlfriends by six people. Their mum or dad's friends, or their friends' parents, were mentioned by another 16 young people. Finally, youth workers were mentioned by four young people. The young people talked about these individuals in very positive terms:

[Friend's mother]...she's like a second ma to me. She's like the da I've never had. (17-year-old female, Scotland)

[Mum's best friend]...it ain't stuff she's done, she's just always been there. (15-year-old female, west of England)

[Youth worker]...various ways really, advice, lending me money...he's offered me work as well. (16-year-old male, south coast)

[Boyfriend's parents]...they are good to sit and talk to. (16-year-old female, Scotland)

Several of the young people said that what was important about these people was that they were always there for them, whatever happened, or whatever they did.

The young people named a variety of things that they would do if they needed some help or advice, or were fed up. Thirteen young people said that they would deal with it themselves, either 'sleep it off' or 'just ignore it', and 'get on with things':

I just bottle it up...[But] it goes away when I have a sleep. (15-year-old female, west of England)

I deal with it myself. (14-year-old male, south coast)

The remainder named other things that they would do in these circumstances. Fourteen said that they would go out with friends, or talk to friends or a best friend. The majority of the sample, 36 young people, said that they would talk to a parent, sibling, or other relative:

I talk to my parents, we all learnt to be open so I talk to my parents about it, they're cool. (15-year-old female, west of England)

If I cannae sort it out myself I will speak to my parents or my boyfriend. (16-year-old female, Scotland)

Me and my mum have got an open relationship and can talk about a lot of things. (15-year-old male, south coast)

Two young people added that they talked to their animals whenever they had a problem:

I talk to the animals because they don't interrupt you...they just listen to you. (13-year-old female, south coast)

[Dog]...he's always there for me when others aren't. (18-year-old female, Scotland)

WHAT DO YOU WORRY ABOUT?

The things that the young people said they worried about were very diverse. One third of the sample – 20 young people – said that they did not worry about anything. Of those who did have worries, many of these were very individual, and named by only one or two people. These included anxieties about ill grandparents, worries about physical health (being too short, worsening arthritis), and being abducted/raped. The other topics that many young people said that they worried about included school work/exams (mentioned by 11 people), the future, in terms of whether they'd get a job or have somewhere to live (named by 13 people), whether they/their family had enough money (named by 25 people), and parental arguments or violence (named by eight people). Comments in response to this question included:

> *Mainly money, how we're all going to cope, how mum and dad are going to react to things, problems that crop up.* (17-year-old female, west of England)

> *That when I'm older I could be poor.* (13-year-old male, Scotland)

> *Everything sometimes, my exams, whether I'll get a job, whether my mum will run out of money. I worry about her a lot.* (14-year-old male, south coast)

It is of particular concern that, as described above, 25 young people said they worried about whether they or their family had enough money to live on.

COMPARISONS WITH OTHER PEOPLE

Two questions in the interview asked the young people about how they thought about their lives in comparison to others. They were asked whether they felt that they were better off, worse off, or about the same as other people, in terms of (i) their enjoyment of life, and (ii) their opportunities for the future.

In terms of how much they enjoy their life, 13 young people thought they were better off than other young people their age. This was because, for example,

> *[I'm better off] because my mum's easy going and nice...I can do things I want.* (13-year-old female, south coast)

> *[I'm better off because] I've got a family who love me, I don't*

need things like alcohol or drugs to make me happy. I'm happy the way I am. (17-year-old female, west of England)

I can't say I'm worse off at all, because I'm not, I'm better off. Look at all the homeless people and those on the streets. It's awful. (15-year-old female, south coast)

Many of the young people who thought they were better off than other young people mentioned other groups in society (in particular the homeless and the elderly) who were worse off than them.

The majority of the young people – 39 young people – believed they were about the same as other young people, in terms of how much they enjoyed their lives. For example:

I'm like most other people, I've got good friends and a nice family. I can't do everything I want to do but then who can? (15-year-old female, south coast)

There's hundreds better off than me, hundreds worse off, so I'm average. (15-year-old female, west of England)

A smaller number – seven young people – believed that they enjoyed their lives much less than other people their age. This was generally because of their lack of money:

I've got no money. (15-year-old female, west of England)

Because you're not having that much fun when you haven't got so much money. (13-year-old male, south coast)

Very similar results were found for the young people's perceptions of their opportunities for the future, in comparison to other young people their age. Thus 11 young people believed they had better opportunities than other young people their age:

I've got goals, I'm doing well at school, my mum supports me, so I'm more likely to do well. (16-year-old female, south coast)

Those believing that their opportunities for the future were average, and the same as those for other people their age, accounted for 38 young people:

Because it all depends how you do at school. (14-year-old male, south coast)

Those believing their opportunities were worse than other young people their age represented nine young people:

> *Because I got in trouble with the law.* (16-year-old male, west of England)

> *It's harder for us to get a job...[because of area he lives in]* (16-year-old male, Scotland)

It is worth noting that the young people's views were often the same in both of these areas – for example believing that they were average, better off or worse off both in terms of their enjoyment in life, and in their opportunities for the future.

EFFECTS OF LIVING ON BENEFITS

In the final part of the interview, the young people were asked whether they felt that being on benefits (and for some living in temporary accommodation) affected how other people viewed or treated them. Two-thirds of the sample – 40 young people – said that they did not think it made any difference to other people's views of them. However, many of these young people also added that most of the people they knew were 'in the same boat', so it was less likely to affect their view of them or treatment of them.

The remaining young people who thought that people did see them differently because they were on benefits or in temporary accommodation, often identified a particular person or group who were negative about them. For example:

- a young man's friends who always laughed at him because he never had enough money to go out;

- two young people who said they were too embarrassed to bring friends back to their house, because it was overcrowded or in very bad condition;

- one young woman who believed her teacher considered she was lazy because no one in her family had a job;

- one young woman believed that her friends felt sorry for her because she didn't have the money for a 'normal' social life;

- one young man believed that, because he lived on an estate where most families were on benefits, people stereotyped him as lazy and unemployable.

These young people also often indicated, as demonstrated in some of these comments, that they felt this affected their prospects, in particular in relation to getting a job.

WHAT WOULD YOU CHANGE IF YOU COULD?

Finally, the young people were asked what they would do if they could change just one thing in their lives. As might be expected, the young people's views on this question were very diverse. However, three themes emerged. First, seven young people said that they would 'do education again', and not be expelled from school or leave without any qualifications. Second, 20 young people wanted things to improve for their parents, such as the ending of domestic violence, having a bigger house, or being able to go on holiday. Third, the most common response (by 28 young people) was to 'win the lottery' and 'have more money', to enable them to pay the family's bills, take the family on holiday, have a better social life, buy a bigger or warmer house, and not to have to 'struggle' for everything. Only a handful of the young people could not think of anything that they would change in their lives.

CHAPTER *10*

Key themes

In the study, four main themes were identified, which ran through each of the areas of the young people's lives described in Chapters 2–9. Each of these themes is described below, using comments from the young people to illustrate the points made.

THEME 1: EARLY AND SIGNIFICANT FAMILY RESPONSIBILITIES

There was clear evidence that a considerable number of the young people in the study had significant family responsibilities, which few young people of their age in other settings would have to bear. These responsibilities took a number of different forms, but two were particularly noticeable.

First, it was shown in Chapter 3 that many of the young people contributed large amounts of their own money to family income, and effectively helped to manage their family's finances. For example:

I give my mum a bit every week just in case she's a bit short and I buy some stuff for the family. (13-year-old male, south coast, in bed and breakfast)

This young man was also opening a bank account with a cash withdrawal card, so that his mother could take money out of his account whenever she needed. Indeed, one reason he gave for getting a part-time job was to be able to contribute to the family income in this way. Many other young people in the study were in the same situation, as has been demonstrated in the young people's comments in the previous chapters:

I give some of [my money] to mum to help her with the shopping because sometimes it's a bit difficult for her so me and my brother help out.

[Interviewer: And your dad, does...]

Oh no, he doesn't know. It might upset him, thinking that she can't manage, so we just keep it between mum, me and my brother. (14-year-old female, south coast)

If I've got enough I give her money and tell her to go out and have a drink or somat or I lends it her. (14-year-old male, west of England)

I try to give [mum] what I can. If it's been a really bad month then I can't, but whenever she's got really bad bills I pay them for her 'cos I know if she doesn't pay them we're gonna get cut off or sent to the courts. (17-year-old male, west of England)

I give her what I can. I'm the oldest and I should help out with them. I'm getting an education and I'll be working soon...they don't have very much money and it's difficult for them to get enough food and pay all the bills. (15-year-old male, south coast)

Many of the young people effectively had no money to spend on themselves, as all their income went to support their family.

The early and significant family responsibilities that many young people had led some young people to plan their futures around the impact of their decisions on their families:

I'll leave [home] when I think it's all right to. When me and my brother get married I think he might move in here or we might get a flat nearby. I don't really wanna leave until I know it's all right to. (14-year-old male, west of England)

This young man was planning to stay nearby in order to ensure that his parents were managing financially. Another young woman described how she was often needed to help with her mother's part-time work, affecting her ability to get on with school work and concentrate on her own future:

[Mum does childminding for extra money]...she needs a lot of help with the babies so if I get home from school and go out she gets really annoyed...I'll come home really tired and she'll tell me to look after them or do something to help...it's really hard work

after a day at school, and I've got homework too. (13-year-old female, south coast)

Many of the young people talked about having to help with their parents' income generation strategies in this way.

Second, it was clear that a significant number of the young people in the study were involved in caring for one or both parents, or in trying to prevent family violence and disagreements. This led to many being distressed, or at risk of physical injury themselves:

I get problems with my nerves when our mum and dad's having a row, I wake up in the morning and my legs and my arms are shaking and that...I was gonna leave the house but I can't leave my [alcoholic] dad in case he gets any problems, so I just came back to the house. (16-year-old male, west of England)

When our dad has a go at our mum, that worries me, if our mum gets up and lashes out at our dad. 'Cos I know if she hits him in the wrong punch he's gonna die. So I don't let our mum hit our dad...I stand in the way, if she hits me she hits me. (16-year-old male, west of England)

A 15-year-old young man described the strain of regularly having to move home on his parents, and how he took the responsibility for that:

It is difficult for them, always packing up. And my mum and dad are getting older now so it's quite hard work, I have to do all the moving of the heavy things, and sorting it all out. (15-year-old male, south coast, bed and breakfast)

It is clear from the above that many of the young people in the study had significant family responsibilities. These included earning money in order to contribute to their families' income, managing and looking after household finances, and looking after parents with health problems or who were strained by bringing up a family on a low income. Further, many of these young people had assumed these responsibilities from a young age, with many of the 13- and 14-year-olds in the study having considerable family responsibilities. This issue is further discussed in the next chapter.

THEME 2: COMPARATIVE SATISFACTION

As was demonstrated in Chapter 9 above, many of the young people in this study believed that they were 'average' or in many ways 'better off' than other young people. This was in many respects a surprising outcome, given the difficulties that many of the young people were experiencing in their lives. A number of young people elaborated on this point, and these views – grouped under the heading of 'comparative satisfaction' – are given here.

A considerable proportion of the young people explained how their circumstances were not as bad as they might first appear. This was because, first, they had such a good relationship with their friends and/or their family. These comments included:

I'm better off than most people because most people are spending their money rotting their liver or blowing their brains out and getting high on drugs. I think I'm better off than any of them, I've got a family who love me, I don't need those things. (17-year-old female, west of England)

Everyone would like more wouldn't they, but that's how it is. I don't think there's anything that I really need that I don't have. My mum says that we should be grateful for what we have, because like we've got a nice family, we all get on, and we've got a nice house and lots of friends. (13-year-old male, south coast)

I think I'm the same as other people but sometimes I think I enjoy it more because I don't get like loads of stuff. I try and enjoy it more, whereas like my friend will get loads and clothes and things all the time. (15-year-old female, south coast)

[Needs anything that hasn't got?]... no, I mean I can always see my friends, and sit and have a beer or a cup of tea here or at their house. You don't really need a lot of money just to relax and see friends do you, it's not essential. (17-year-old male, south coast)

Second, other young people, in particular those in bed and breakfast, focused on the advantages or good points about living in the circumstances that they were:

[Same as others because]...we can get out and do stuff. We can't

have people back to [the hotel] but we can go out and do stuff,
like go swimming or down the park. I wouldn't say that we've got
the best life but like people go 'I wish I could do that, it's a hotel
so you get your breakfast each morning' and things like that.
(13-year-old male, south coast, bed and breakfast)

A few of the young people seemed to try hard to find something in their lives that they could say was good, a part that other people might be envious of ('everyone needs to feel good about something', as one young woman said).

Third, several of the young people reflected more generally on why some people are on a low income, and concluded that this was simply the way life was, and that they couldn't do anything about it. They should therefore accept what they have. As one young person said:

Well that's just how it is. I don't think it's wrong. People are born
into different circumstances, you know some people have a lot of
money and some people don't have very much, and we don't
have very much...that's just how it is. (17-year-old male, south coast)

Many of the young people made comments like these.

This notion – of being better off, or not as badly off, as some other people – is described as 'comparative satisfaction' in this report. This is because many of the young people, whilst being aware that their lives were difficult, often mentioned that they were not as difficult as some people's lives – the homeless, those without friends, and those with poor family relationships. Thus, compared to others, they were fairly satisfied with their lives.

It is interesting to note, in fact, that several of the young people disputed the use of the word 'poverty' to describe their situation. Reflecting the varying definitions of poverty given in Chapter 1, several young people said that their family were not living in poverty. Poverty, many suggested, referred to those people who were completely destitute, in particular the homeless. It did not apply to people like them, people who were 'getting by'. They were, as several young people said, 'poor', 'hard up', and people who 'don't have much to live on'. This is an interesting contribution to the debate about the nature of poverty, which was discussed in Chapter 1.

THEME 3: THE IMPACT OF A LIMITED INCOME ON YOUNG PEOPLE

The results presented in the main part of this report explored, in key areas, the impact of a limited income on young people. However, there were a number of issues in relation to this, which cut across all the eight areas described, and these are discussed here.

First, many of the young people talked about the way in which, whatever they did or wanted to do, they always had to think about money first. This was, for many, one of the most difficult aspects of growing up on a low income. For example:

> For me it's about not being part of things, not having the money to live normally like other people. Everything I do or I want to do, even like really small things, is decided by money, or by not having it anyway. (14-year-old female, west of England)

> We've had to pay bills off and we're forever living on credit cards and things like that but we can't afford to. You always have to think 'how are we going to pay for this?' (14-year-old female, west of England)

> [I miss]...just the freedom to say on the spot you can do things. Because if someone says do you want to go out or there's a school trip you have to check you can afford it...you can't spontaneously do things. You have to work out if you've got the money and then maybe ask to borrow some...which is difficult. (17-year-old female, south coast)

Many of the older young people in the sample, the 16- to 18-year-olds, said that it was more difficult to be on a low income now they were older. As one young person said:

> I'd really like to travel you know, go somewhere different. It's worse now 'cos my friends are starting to go away as a group, to Butlins or to Malta and stuff, and I could never do that...it's different now because of my age, I want to go out and do things, and I'd like to start getting more up-to-date clothes and that sort of thing.

[Interviewer: So it was different when you were younger?]

*Oh yeah I didn't mind then, I didn't do that much. I was happy
watching TV, taking the dogs out. But now I'm older, I'm nearly an
adult and the things I want to do cost money which I don't have.*
(17-year-old female, south coast)

Others in the 16–18 age range described how having little or no
money affected everything that they wanted to do at that age – going
out, seeing friends, buying things – and also their prospects for the
future, in terms of experiences of and access to education, training and
employment. One young woman described being poor as a 'vicious
circle', where everywhere you turn you find 'closed doors'.

Secondly, the young people often talked about the difficulty of
maintaining good relationships with family and friends when living on
a limited income, and how this was a major aspect of growing up in
poverty. This was because, for example, they couldn't afford to travel
to see friends and family who lived a distance away, or couldn't afford
to join in leisure and social activities with other people. This was particularly noticeable for many of the young people who lived in isolated
rural areas in the west of England sample; here lack of money was
exacerbated by the lack of transport available. It was also particularly
difficult to maintain relationships with friends when the family did not
have a phone, which was most common amongst those in temporary
accommodation and those living in very rural areas. Also, lack of
money also affected relationships within the family, often leading to
arguments within the home. For example

*My little brother doesn't understand. He wants more money and
more clothes...he gets really angry with mum and dad. So I give
my brother something, if I've got it.* (14-year-old female, south coast)

*I shouldn't I know, it's not their fault, but I just want things, like
things other people have got, and I just go on, you know asking if I
can them, and they just get really fed up with me.* (13-year-old
female, south coast)

Many described how they tried to keep their frustration 'bottled up',
but that at times it just 'burst out'.

The impact of a low income on the young people's relationships
with their families was often therefore revealed in quite subtle ways.
Although initially the majority of the young people said they had good

relationships with their parents (see Chapter 5) tensions and difficulties often arose, many of which were related to income. As the quotes above demonstrate, many of the young people felt acutely frustrated about the limitations that a low income imposed, and this often led to disagreements and arguments. For many young people this was exacerbated by living in bed and breakfast accommodation or in homes with insufficient space (see Chapter 2).

THEME 4: THE IMPORTANCE OF FAMILY RELATIONSHIPS

It was demonstrated earlier in this report that many young people felt that, although living on a limited income was very hard, it was made easier by having close family and personal relationships. This was a theme that many of the young people often referred to. The young people described this in a number of different ways, such as

> *I don't need anything really. As long as I've got love off my parents and support, things like that. I think that's more important than radios and things like that...It's more important to have support.* (14-year-old female, south coast)

Others compared their lives to those of people they knew who, although better off materially and financially than they were, had poor family relationships:

> *My friend up the road...her mum and dad just give her TV and stuff like that...but she doesn't actually get any real love off them.* (15-year-old female, south coast)

It is of note that the relatively small group of young people in the study who seemed particularly depressed about their lives, and who were often most pessimistic about the future, also commented on their poor relationship with their families.

Much other work on this topic has identified the important role of good personal relationships as a 'buffer' against living in difficult circumstances, such as poverty. The results of the research described here give added support to this, with the young people clearly articulating how their good family relationships acted to make their lives enjoyable and meaningful, and made them feel valued and loved. However, one consequence of this is a clear sense of young people 'putting up with' their difficult lives, accepting that it is just 'the way it is' that some families live in poverty. Without the love and support of their families, however, it is clear that many of the young people in this study would find their lives a great deal more difficult.

This is an important issue, which we return to in the following chapter.

CHAPTER 11

Conclusions and policy recommendations

This report has addressed the issue of young people growing up in family poverty. It aimed to provide information about a neglected group of young people – those living with their families and growing up in poverty. In particular, the research aimed to focus on young people and young people's words to describe their lives, and their experience of growing up with a limited income.

This final chapter of the report aims to do a number of things. First, there is a general summary of the main findings of the research. Second, the influence of key variables – gender, ethnicity, age, and locality – is explored. Third, the implications of the study for research in this area are outlined, including a discussion of the methodological issues and directions for future research that arise from it. Fourth and finally, a number of policy recommendations are made, addressing the ways in which specific policy changes could help to improve the quality of life, and the prospects, of young people who are growing up in family poverty.

SUMMARY OF THE MAIN FINDINGS

A considerable amount of information was collected in the research and the key results are summarised below.

Chapter 2 demonstrated that the majority of the young people were living in council-owned accommodation and privately rented accommodation. Whilst a minority of the young people were positive about their homes, a considerable number lived in damp and cold accommodation, or accommodation in need of repair. Many of the young people did not have enough rooms to accommodate their family properly, many using a lounge for people to sleep in. Lack of space became more problematic with age. Further, many of the young people's homes were in areas with a poor reputation, which many felt made people react adversely to them.

Chapter 2 also included information about the young people's parents, notably their employment history and income. The majority of the parents had not worked since the young people had been born, especially the mothers. Two-thirds of the young people did not know how much money their parents had coming in to the house, although all knew that their parents were living on benefits. There was evidence that at least a quarter of the families also had money coming in from other sources, including part-time work. There was a considerable amount of fluidity in many families' incomes.

Chapter 3 explored the young people's own income. The majority had £10 or less to spend each week, with a number of young people having no income at all. Those who did have an income received it from a variety of sources, but mainly from pocket money or part-time work, with a number also involved in illegal activities. Few young people had any savings. It became clear that many of the young people contributed all or part of their income to help support their family financially, whereas others did not receive any money at all from their parents, as a way of contributing to family finances.

Chapter 4 explored the impact of their family's circumstances and a low income on young people's friends and social lives. This particularly affected young people living in bed and breakfast accommodation (who had often been moved away from friends when re-housed, and who did not have anywhere to bring friends back to), and those in rural areas (where the costs of transport to see friends were often prohibitive). Some of those in poor quality accommodation described themselves as too embarrassed to bring anyone back to their homes. The difficulties of maintaining friendships and having a social life when on a low income was clearly acknowledged by many of the young people, who often talked about being bored and stuck in a routine where they didn't do anything.

Chapter 5 described the family composition and family relationships of the sample. Almost half of the sample were living in single-parent households, with the remainder living with their natural parents and in step-families. More than one third of the sample had no contact at all with a natural parent, generally their father. Relationships with mothers and step-mothers were generally rated as better than relationships with fathers and step-fathers. Very few young people identified their limited income as a factor that affected their relationship with their parents; however, further probing showed that for many young people income was a source of tension and disagreement.

Chapter 6 examined the physical health of the sample. This chapter demonstrated, crucially, that the young people had very subjective views about what counted as good or poor health. However, two-thirds of the sample described their health as average or OK. Although a majority of young people said that their families' income did not affect the food they ate, many then demonstrated numerous ways in which they often went without food, ate poor quality food, and had an unvaried diet. In terms of substance use, almost half of the sample were regular smokers, most commonly in the Scottish and west of England samples. Most had started to smoke from a young age. Further, a majority of the young people lived in homes where one and sometimes two or more people smoked. In terms of alcohol use, there were a number of heavy drinkers in the study, again mostly in the Scottish and west of England samples. Similarly, these two areas included the majority of the 20 young people who were regular users of illegal drugs.

Chapter 7 detailed the young people's experience of education, their current status, and future plans. A number of young people (one third of the total sample) had (or were having) very poor experiences in education. This included being bullied, falling behind, and having literacy problems; many also described their acute dislike of education and being at school. Several of the young people had been excluded from school, or had been persistent non-attenders. A significant number of this group, however, now regretted leaving school early and/or with no skills or qualifications, and were trying to get back into education. The young people named a variety of jobs that they would like to have in the future, but most were not optimistic that they would be able to achieve these goals.

Chapter 8 described the young people's involvement in and experiences of crime and the law. Over half of the sample had been involved in crime, with 16 young people involved in very serious offences. Many of this group identified their criminal activity as stemming from boredom, lack of money to do the things that they wanted to do, and also as a result of the illegal activities of friends and family. Over half of the sample had family and/or friends who were or who had been involved in crime. Finally, this chapter demonstrated that more than a third of the young people had been victims of crime.

Chapter 9 focused on some of the more personal and psychological effects of growing up in family poverty. It showed that the young people had very diverse perceptions of their lives, ranging from those who were extremely positive to those who were very negative. Similarly, there was a range of views about the future, although the majority said they were 'very optimistic'; however, many were only optimistic if certain things were to happen, such as managing to get a job, or getting back into education. Two-thirds of the young people identified a key individual outside their family who they believed had been helpful and supportive to them as they were growing up. Finally, this chapter identified that a majority of the young people felt that their enjoyment of life was the same or better than anyone else; similar results were found for the young people's view of their opportunities for the future. Only a small group of young people, generally in Scotland and the west of England, felt they were worse off on both these questions.

Finally, Chapter 10 identified a number of key themes which arose throughout the interviews with the young people. These were: (i) that many of the young people had early and significant family responsibilities, for example contributing to family income or acting as a carer within the family; (ii) that there was evidence of comparative satisfaction, of many young people believing that their lives were good in comparison to other groups of people, such as the homeless; (iii) that the impact of a limited income was found in all areas of their lives, and often revealed itself in subtle ways; and (iv) that good family relationships 'buffered' many of the young people from the more debilitating effects of growing up in family poverty.

INFLUENCE OF KEY VARIABLES IN THE RESEARCH

One of the aims of the research was to explore the influence of four key variables on young people's experience of growing up in family poverty – gender, ethnicity, age and locality. The findings in relation to these variables are described here, although it should be remembered that this was a relatively small sample of 60 young people. Further research is needed to see if the findings apply in larger populations.

First, in terms of gender, there were relatively few differences found between the young men and young women in any of the areas explored in the interview. The only area where a gender difference was found was in relation to involvement in crime, where twice as many young men as young women were currently (or had been) involved in crime. This finding is consistent with national figures for the involvement of young people in crime (see Coleman, 1997). Also, more of the young men had been excluded or were absent from school; again this reflects national figures (Coleman, 1997). Apart from these two aspects, however, there were few differences between the young men and young women in this study. The results of this study, therefore, suggest that the experience of poverty is very similar for young men and young women.

Second, firm conclusions about the experiences of different ethnic groups are difficult to make, because of the small numbers involved – only seven ethnic minority young people were included in the study. This is in itself an important issue, in that researchers in all three areas found it very difficult to recruit ethnic minority young people to participate, in particular young people from Asian families.

A number of youth workers and social workers, and young people, said that there was a greater stigma attached in many ethnic minority groups to being dependent on state benefits, and also greater fears about confidentiality and the uses of the material collected. Of those ethnic minority young people who did participate in the study (just over 10 per cent of the whole sample), there were no clear differences between them and the white/European young people involved. However, it is possible that the questioning was not sufficiently sensitive to the experiences of ethnic minority young people living in poverty, and that differences that do exist were not picked up in the interviews. Also, no ethnic minority interviewers were involved, which may have affected the responses of this group of young people. This is an important area for future research to address.

The main differences identified in the study were in terms of the two variables of (third) age and (fourth) locality. In terms of the third variable, age, it was clear throughout the study that the older groups felt the effects of growing up in poverty most acutely. Thus poverty was found to affect young people's friendships and social lives, leisure activities, and need for privacy and personal space. Before this age, it was clear that the impact of poverty was not as acute, with the exception of the significant family responsibilities identified, which were found across the age range. This is a particularly important finding, because as demonstrated in Chapter 1, most research has focused on the effects of poverty on young children. Yet this research shows that the effects of poverty on young people (particularly older young people) are very acute.

Fourth, the different geographical areas and locations that the young people lived in was found to make a difference to their experience of poverty. This was demonstrated by a number of the areas explored, and most commonly distinguished those young people living on the south coast with those from the west of England and Scotland, and sometimes the south coast and west of England samples from the Scottish young people. The south coast sample, despite including seven young people in temporary and bed and breakfast accommodation, were generally the most positive and optimistic of all the young people, and those who were doing best in education. They were also less likely to be those who were involved in crime, and less likely to smoke or use illegal drugs.

There are a number of possible explanations for the differences found in the study in terms of locality. One is that the young people in the south coast and some of the west of England samples were mainly living in mixed areas, in terms of housing, social backgrounds of residents, and rates of crime and unemployment. The young people in the Scottish sample, however, were living mainly on large run-down estates, experiencing multiple problems and were exposed to high levels of crime, gang violence, unemployment and drug use. It is possible, therefore, that the Scottish young people were experiencing higher levels of deprivation, and also that there were fewer 'buffers' to protect them from the negative consequences of their environment.

Similarly, the differences found for the west of England sample were often related to the rural nature of the environment that many of the young people lived in – such as difficulties in accessing employment and training, and problems in getting to see friends and to socialise (see Davis and Ridge, 1997; Derounian, 1993 for a discussion of these points). It was therefore seen as an important decision to include young people from different geographical locations in the study (see the following section for further discussion of this point). However, it is also important to remember that this was a qualitative study, and that the numbers involved in each area were small. Further research is needed on a larger sample to discover whether these differences are generalisable.

IMPLICATIONS FOR RESEARCH INTO YOUNG PEOPLE AND POVERTY

This report has described research into the experiences of young people growing up in family poverty. As stated above, it was considered important to focus on young people's own words and experiences in reporting their experiences of poverty, to include young people from a range of backgrounds, and to explore the effects of poverty on a wide range of areas of young people's lives.

The research also has a number of implications for future work in this area. There are both lessons to be learnt from the research, as well as questions raised by it, which need to be addressed in the future. These are briefly described here.

First, there were a number of important groups who were not included in the research, whose experience of growing up in poverty might be very different to that described here. These include young people with disabilities, young people who are pregnant or who have children, and those from ethnic minority groups which were not represented in the research. It is possible that young people in these circumstances have very different experiences of growing up in families living in poverty. These groups need to be targeted in future research.

Second, researchers are often debating the value of quantitative as opposed to qualitative research with young people. The research described here showed the value of qualitative research methods in exploring the topics concerned. It is of note that, although this research used individual qualitative interviews, a number of quantitative measures were also included in the study. The quantitative results are not given in this report, however, because some of the findings were inconsistent or misleading. For example, one of the quantitative measures (using a questionnaire that the young people completed themselves) asked whether they had experienced a series of different 'life events' over the last year, including whether they had experienced a 'long period of illness'. This item was intended to discover whether the young people had had any serious or long-term illnesses. However, it was clear that many young people were answering 'yes' on this question, meaning that they had had 'flu for a week during the previous year, when they were the sort of person who was not normally ill. This for them was a 'long period of illness'. Examples of different interpretations of quantitative questions such as that described above, led the author to conclude that qualitative methods, in particular individual interviews, are appropriate methods for researching the complex and sensitive topics described here. It was essential that those collecting the information were able to prompt, clarify, question and explore the young people's responses.

Third, and related to the above point, is the importance for future research to focus on young people's subjective meanings and own words in describing their lives. This acknowledges young people's right to speak for themselves about their lives, and also allows them to explain and elucidate their views about the things that affect them. The research described here aimed to focus on young people's perspectives, and to present the information in their words as much as possible. Future research might well use other approaches to extend and develop this work, using other methods to enable young people's voices to be heard. This might include the use of photographic and video methodologies, as well as enabling young people to undertake and disseminate the research themselves.

Fourth, one of the issues to emerge very clearly in this research was young people's resilience. It was also clear that many young people were accepting what they have, even in the most difficult and frustrating circumstances. Issues around resilience and coping have only very recently become a focus for research. A renewed effort is needed in this area, combined with a focus on understanding young people's subjective experiences, as described above. In making this suggestion, the author agrees with the American researchers Wilson *et al.* (1997), who conclude from their study of low income youth in the United States that

> It is important for professionals who work with low-income youth
> to become more aware of and sensitive to how a person's

'interpretation' of his/her circumstances function to modify the meaning and experience of life satisfaction...[this] does not provide the basis for neglecting obvious deficiencies in the objective conditions of [these young people]. Instead, reports of high life satisfaction in the face of adversity may simply reflect the resilience of youth from low-income backgrounds through the development of coping mechanisms and the lowering of expectations in the face of seemingly insurmountable obstacles. (Wilson *et al.*, 1997, p. 457)

The relationship between life circumstances, resilience, coping, and life expectations is an important area for future research to address.

Fifth and finally, a key recommmendation for future research is for longitudinal studies of the effects of poverty on young people. The research described here is essentially a 'snapshot' at a particular point in the lives of 60 young people who are growing up in family poverty. This clearly raises questions about what will happen to these young people in the future. Longitudinal research is therefore needed to answer key questions arising from this study, such as:

- What happens to the young people in this study who are involved in crime, or excluded from school? Are there factors that lead them away from crime or back into education?

- What happens to these young people long-term in terms of employment, training, or unemployment?

- How do these young people's family relationships change over time?

- When do the young people leave home, and how does this affect their relationship with their families?

- What are the long-term health behaviours and outcomes of these young people?

- How do resilience and coping develop and change over time? To what extent does young people's sense of optimism or pessimism in the teenage years change in early adulthood?

These and other important questions need to be addressed by following young people such as these through into adulthood.

IMPLICATIONS FOR YOUTH POLICY

The title of this report – 'Worth More Than This' – was chosen to reflect the author's belief that young people should not have to spend their teenage years struggling and 'making do', in the way that many of the young people in the study were. The primary aim of the research was to highlight and publicise these young people's experiences, and to document the effects on young people of growing up in family poverty. The aim was to focus on young people's words, and to focus on young people's subjective experiences.

There are clear issues raised by the research described here, all of which have policy implications. These are detailed, briefly, below. The list is not exhaustive – indeed, a whole book could be written about youth policy. However it is believed that, if the policy recommendations below were followed, the circumstances and future prospects of some of the most disadvantaged young people in our society could be vastly improved.

1. A change in the conceptualisation of poverty in the 1990s

The results of this study have implications for the way in which policy-makers, politicians and the public view poverty. It was suggested in Chapter 1 that there is an ongoing debate in this country about what exactly poverty is. The young people in this study demonstrate that, whilst many may not be living in complete destitution, they are living in poverty. In this definition, poverty means living life as a struggle, making sacrifices, putting up with less than someone wants to or is entitled to, and the lowering of horizons and expectations.

Most of the young people in this study were experiencing 'poverty by exclusion', as described by Smith (1990) and others (Child Poverty Action Group, 1993a; Kumar, 1993). Using this conceptualisation of poverty, the urgency of tackling this issue is apparent. 'Poverty' has re-appeared on the political and public agenda in the late 1990s. It is essential that the new Social Exclusion Unit, set up by the Prime Minister in 1998, should address the important issues described here.

2. Changes to family income and benefit policies

The present Labour government is currently in the process of reviewing policies relating to social security and benefits. It was clear that many of the families who participated in this research were struggling to survive on the current level of benefits. Even a relatively small increase in benefit levels would make a considerable amount of difference to most of these families. As a recent Rowntree-funded study demonstrated, an additional £15 a week would greatly improve the ability of many of those living on very low incomes to cope (Kempson, 1996).

An increase in benefit payments to these families might also mean that young people, particularly the 13- and 14-year-olds, would not have to contribute part or all of their income to their parents, in order to help them survive. Changes in benefit levels for these families should also include the restoration of benefits to those aged 16 and 17 who are not in education or training. Without these benefits, several of this age group in the study were left with no income at all.

3. Increased provision of youth and leisure services

It was clear that many of the young people in this study experienced acute boredom, mainly because they were unable to afford to participate in many leisure activities. Many of the young people described the importance of youth clubs and youth workers in their lives, which provided them with leisure facilities, friendship, advice and guidance. There must be a greater expenditure on the youth service and the provision of inexpensive leisure activities for young people.

The costs of not doing this are clear from the young people in this report – many described how boredom and lack of leisure activities led them to get involved in crime and substance abuse. The cost-effectiveness of this policy in the long-term has been clearly demonstrated by the *Misspent Youth* report (Audit Commission, 1996). A greater commitment to the youth service and inexpensive leisure activities for young people would be a key investment for the future.

4. The importance of education

Many of the young people in this study, in particular those who were involved in crime, had had very negative experiences of education. It is important that more attention is given to those who 'slip through the net' as many of these young people did, in particular through literacy problems and falling behind at school. Further, the 1990s have witnessed a dramatic increase in school exclusions, a fact that (as has already been demonstrated) is associated with unemployment and involvement in crime.

It is also clear from this study that more 'second chances' are needed, providing opportunities for those who have been excluded or who left school early to return to education. There are a number of important and innovative projects currently underway, but these are few in number, and funding for them is scarce. Education is central to improving young people's futures and prospects, a fact very clearly recognised by all the young people in this study.

5. Improving youth employment prospects

A significant number of the young people in this study felt it was difficult to motivate themselves through education and training, because of the high rates of youth unemployment in the UK at present. Many felt that, however hard they worked, the prospects of ever getting a job were poor. This made many feel that there was little point in gaining qualifications or undertaking training.

Policies are therefore needed which improve the employment prospects for young people, and to address seriously the issue of youth unemployment. This research was undertaken before the present government's New Deal programme was set up, and it is unclear at present how successful this will be in tackling youth unemployment. However, a clear outcome from this study is a need for the provision of more training and employment opportunities for young people, in particular those who have had poor experiences of education.

CONCLUSION

This report has focused on understanding the lives of some of the most disadvantaged young people in British society. The title of the report – 'Worth More Than This' – was chosen with care. Young people are the future, and are worth the investment. The consequences of not addressing the policy issues highlighted above are clear – increases in youth alienation, crime, substance abuse, ill health and disaffection.

It is hoped that the words of the young people described here will make a difference. It is appropriate to end this report with some of the comments from the young people, which sum up the urgency of the issues:

For me [being poor is] about not being part of things, not having the money to live normally like other people. Everything I do or I want to do, even like really small things, is decided by money, or by not having it anyway. (14-year-old female)

I try not to complain, sometimes I feel guilty you know, but it is hard being poor, you're just surviving, not really living. Sometimes the future seems, like, hard you know, it just feels it'll be such a struggle. I just hope it won't be as bad for us in the future as it is now. (16-year-old female)

This report is dedicated to all young people who are Worth More Than This.

References

Alcock, P. (1993) *Understanding Poverty*. London: Macmillan.

Audit Commission (1996) *Misspent Youth*. London: Audit Commission.

Balding, J. (1996) *Young People in 1995*. Exeter: Schools Health Education Unit.

Barnardo's (1995) *Doing Time: Families Living in Temporary Accommodation in London*. Ilford: Barnardo's.

Becker, S. (Ed.) (1991) *Windows of Opportunity: Public Policy and the Poor*. London: Child Poverty Action Group.

Blackburn, C. (1991) *Poverty and Health*. OUP: Milton Keynes.

Brannen, J., Dodd, K., Oakley, A., Storey, P. (1994) *Young People, Health and Family Life*. Buckingham: Open University Press.

British Medical Association (1995) *Inequalities in Health*. London: British Medical Association.

British Youth Council (1993) *The Time of Your Life?: The Truth about Being Young in 90s Britain*. London: British Youth Council.

Catan, L., Dennison, C., Coleman, J. (1996) *Effective Communication in the Teenage Years*. London: The BT Forum.

Clark, A. (1996) 'Policy and provision for the schooling of children living in temporary accommodation.' *Children and Society*, vol. 10, pp. 293–304.

Coleman, C. (1997) *Key Data on Adolescence*. Brighton: Trust for the Study of Adolescence.

COYPSS (1993) *Young People and Severe Hardship*. London: COYPSS (Coalition on Young People and Social Security).

Cullingford, C., Morrison, J. (1997) Peer group pressure within and outside the school. *British Educational Research Journal*, vol. 23, pp. 61–80.

Davis, J., Ridge, T. (1997) *Same Scenery, Different Lifestyle: Rural Children on a Low Income*. London: The Children's Society.

Dennehy, A., Smith, L., Harker, P. (1997) *Not to be Ignored: Young People, Poverty, and Health*. London: Child Poverty Action Group.

Derounian, J. G. (1993) *Another Country: Real Life Beyond Rose Cottage*. London: National Council for Voluntary Organisations.

Emler, N., Reicher, S. D. (1995) *The Social Psychology of Adolescent Delinquency*. Oxford: Blackwell.

Hertfordshire County Council (1996) *Anti-Poverty Action Plan*. Hertford: HCC.

Holman, B. (1994) 'Research review: Children and poverty.' *Children and Society*, vol. 8, pp. 69–72.

Kempson, E. (1996) *Life On A Low Income*. York: Joseph Rowntree Trust.

Kumar, V. (1993) *Poverty and Inequality in the UK: The Effects on Children*. London: National Children's Bureau.

Long, G., MacDonald, S., Scott, G. (1996) *Child and Family Poverty in Scotland: The Facts*. Glasgow: Glasgow Caledonian University.

National Youth Agency (1996) *Briefing: Poverty – The Facts*. Leicester: NYA.

National Children's Home (1993a) *A Lost Generation? A Survey of the Problems Faced by Vulnerable Young People Living on Their Own*. London: National Children's Home.

National Children's Home (1993b) *Your Place or Mine?* London: National Children's Home.

Oldfield, N., Yu, A. (1993) *The Cost of a Child: Living Standards for the 1990s*. London: Child Poverty Action Group.

Oppenheim, C. (1993a) *Poverty: The Facts*. London: Child Poverty Action Group.

Oppenheim, C. (1993b) *Families and the Recession: Living on the Breadline*. London: Child Poverty Action Group.

Roll, J. (1992) *Understanding Poverty: A Guide to Concepts and Measures*. London: Family Policy Studies Centre.

Smith, R. (1990) *Working With Families: Tackling Poverty*. London: The Children's Society.

Utting, D,, Bright, J., Henricson, C. (1993) *Crime and the Family*. London: Family Policy Studies Centre.

Wilson, S., Henry, C., Petersen, G. (1997) 'Life satisfaction among low-income rural youth from Appalachia.' *Journal of Adolescence*, vol. 20, pp. 443–460.

THE CHILDREN'S SOCIETY
A POSITIVE FORCE FOR CHANGE

The Children's Society is one of Britain's leading charities for children and young people. Founded in 1881 as a Christian organisation, The Children's Society reaches out unconditionally to children and young people regardless of race, culture or creed.

Over 90 projects throughout England and Wales
We work with over 30,000 children of all ages, focusing on those whose circumstances have made them particularly vulnerable. We aim to help stop the spiral into isolation, anger and lost hope faced by so many young people.

We constantly look for effective, new ways of making a real difference
We measure local impact and demonstrate through successful practice that major issues can be tackled and better resolved. The Children's Society has an established track record of taking effective action: both in changing public perceptions about difficult issues such as child prostitution, and in influencing national policy and practice to give young people a better chance at life.

The Children's Society is committed to overcoming injustice wherever we find it
We are currently working towards national solutions to social isolation, lack of education and the long-term problems they cause, through focused work in several areas:

- helping parents whose babies and toddlers have inexplicably stopped eating, endangering their development;
- involving children in the regeneration of poorer communities;
- preventing exclusions from primary and secondary schools;
- providing a safety net for young people who run away from home and care;
- seeking viable alternatives to the damaging effects of prison for young offenders.

The Children's Society will continue to raise public awareness of difficult issues to promote a fairer society for the most vulnerable children in England and Wales. For further information about the work of The Children's Society or to obtain a publications catalogue, please contact:
The Publishing Department, The Children's Society, Edward Rudolf House, Margery Street, London WC1X 0JL. Tel. 0171 837 4299. Fax 0171 837 0211.

The Children's Society is a registered charity: Charity Registration No. 221124.